The Idea Generator

Quick and Easy Kaizen

Bunji Tozawa
Norman Bodek

Edited by Shelly Rivoli and Beth Simone

Parts of The Idea Generator was originally published March 1999 in Japanese under the title of Quick and Easy Work Improvement Seminar Basics by Nikkan Kogyo Shimbunsha in a special addition of Kojo Kanri magazine.

PCS Inc.
809 S.E. 73rd Avenue
Vancouver, WA 98664

360-737-1883
360-737-1940 fax
bodek@pcspress.com

Printed in the United States of America

Printing number
1 2 3 4 5 6 7 8 9 10

Library of Congress Cataloging-in-publication Data

Tozawa, Bunji and Bodek, Norman.
    The Idea Generator – Quick and Easy Kaizen / Bunji Tozawa and Norman Bodek.

    p. cm.
    Includes index.

    ISBN 0-9712436-9-7
    1. Customer service.   2. Industrial management.
    3. Production management.   4. Organizational change.
    5. Organizational behavior.   I. Title.
       2001

This book is dedicated to the
Universal Energy
that has imparted to every
individual a very unique
creative spirit from which we
can all draw upon to evolve
and grow infinitely.

Acknowledgements

This book is a collaborative project containing a methodology that has evolved over many years. As we state in the book, Kodak is credited with establishing the first idea system in 1898 to get employees involved in making improvements. But somehow the system switched from its initial intentions of being an employee involvement system to become in America a cost saving suggestion system.

Someone in Japan in the late 1960s early 1970s re-examined the American suggestion system and went back and re-applied the original system as created by Kodak. Over the last thirty to forty years the idea system has matured, evolved and been perfected to become a very powerful management tool. The Quick and Easy Kaizen system, as explained in this book, we believe synthesizes the very latest thinking and best application of an idea process that is currently used by world-class companies both in Japan and in America.

We particularly acknowledge, with gratitude, the support and cooperation of the employees of the Dana Corporation, one of the world's largest automotive parts suppliers, who have successfully applied the ideas in this book throughout their company. We especially thank Joe Magliochetti, CEO, Tony Shelbourn, VP Corp. Relations, Gary Corrigan, VP Corporate Communications, Pat Pilleri, Plant Manager, Mark Anderson and JB McCarthy – Manufacturing Managers, Structural Products Division in Hopkinsville, KY, John Leech, General Manager in the American Electronics Components Division, Dan Cavanagh, Plant Manager in Stockton, CA, Jack Simms, EIM Coordinator in Statesville, NC and all of the other great people at Dana who shared their ideas with us.

I want to thank M. G. Gaston, Debi Moniz, Arlene D. Martinez and the other members if their team at NUUMI for sharing their wonderful ideas.

I want to thank Shelly Rivoli for editing the book and to Beth Simone who proof read and also edited the book, William Christopher for constant encouragement and support, Da-Wei (David) Yu for his insight in always seeing the strategic approach, Tsuey Hwa Lai for her ideas on design, Christo Gorawski cartoonist, Shana O'Brien for her tying skills, also Irv Otis, Lee Gillis, T. V. Suresh for their valuable advice, and to my lovely wife Noriko Hosoyamada who translated from Japanese to English Bunji Tozawa's material.

I want to thank the following successful authors for their kindness in reviewing the book: Richard J. Schonberger, Min Basadur, Jeffrey K. Liker, Jac Fitz-Enz, and Greg Hutchins

And I want to thank all of the great people whose quotes I used throughout the book with special thanks and appreciation to my eternal teacher Rudi.

I give special thanks to my co-author Bunji Tozawa who has graciously allowed me to share his expertise with America and the western world.

Norman Bodek

"THE IDEA GENERATOR"

Foreword

Back in the early 1990s, I participated in a very rewarding study mission to Japan led by Norman Bodek, co-author of *The Idea Generator*. The original thought behind the trip was to provide a number of key managers from our company, the Dana Corporation, with an opportunity to personally benchmark some of the most advanced productivity methods anywhere in the world.

But as you will learn on the pages that follow, an idea unleashed can often spur additional, unanticipated benefits. Looking back today, that trip to Japan also served as the catalyst for the creation of Dana's Idea Program, which has subsequently become a centerpiece of our corporate culture. Through our experiences in Japan, we established the framework for a program that has enabled our company to tap into its full resources by involving our people at all levels of the organization directly in enhancing and improving the total productivity of our operations.

Another interesting fact we gleaned from that visit to Japan, is the exponential impact that can be derived from an idea. Certainly we've experienced this dynamic within Dana. Through modifying a process that perhaps makes their job a little easier, our people also improve the quality and efficiency of the products produced through their efforts. This phenomenon has a wonderful way of making people feel further motivated, and they generally enjoy greater recognition as a result of their efforts. And as people see their ideas reflected in the operations of the company, new ideas are stimulated.

Another major benefit of our idea system has surfaced in the realm of customer service. Through this program, we've worked to uncover additional ways in which we can eliminate waste in the system –both at our end, as well as in our customer's place of business. In fact, we've often had workers from our plants visit the customer in order to view the *next* step in the process. The result is frequently an improvement in the way we deliver the product. By asking customer-focused questions, we are able to use our idea program to develop solutions. Is delivery direct to the customer's line? Is it in a quantity that's handy for them to move about in their facilities? Is there a way we can protect the product so there are fewer defects upon installation? Each of these topics is a by-product of the idea program and has helped Dana serve its customers more effectively.

We find that the people who are the most prolific in their ideas and in their involvement are the most satisfied as well. In addition to our people feeling better about their contributions, many of our facilities have gain-sharing programs in place. The system varies by location, but in general, when we can reduce the cost of producing the product, we are willing to share that gain with our people on what we believe is a fair and equitable basis. Again, this further reflects the broader value of an idea unleashed.

While some idea programs focus on manufacturing gains, the concept is equally applicable to support functions such as sales, accounting, engineering, and customer service. Supervisors and managers also participate, though it's interesting that this was an area that initially required some prompting to convince our people to document their ideas. As supervisors, many of our people thought that coming up with creative solutions and implementing them was just part of their job. But, what we are also trying to do is to expand each person's horizon of thought beyond just his or her own 25 square feet of workspace. We'd like to improve the entire work process. So, if our people see something that is adjacent to their immediate assignment that can be improved by helping a colleague or by changing the workflow, we want to address that opportunity as well.

Ideas like these have worked particularly well in another Dana program, something we refer to as the Dana Quality Leadership Process (DQLP). The DQLP is basically fashioned after the Malcolm Baldrige National Quality Award criteria, which emphasizes the benefits of diligently recording process improvements and constantly working to verify and validate that the improvements are achieved, and that best practices are reflected throughout our operations. By benchmarking others, we are able to challenge our own methodologies to improve even further. This type of documentation and detail is certainly one of the contributing factors in two Dana operations having earned the prestigious Baldrige award.

There is more benchmarking taking place in business today than ever before. At Dana, we have a wide variety of people who come through our facilities to learn more about our idea program – including people like Mr. Bodek and his co-author, Mr. Tozawa, who are kind enough to document and distribute the ideas to stimulate additional interest.

However, there are still many companies that choose not to leverage the full resources available to them. Still others balk at programs focusing on idea generation and education, citing the cost involved. Our response to this has typically been that while these programs do require investment, this expense pales in comparison to the cost of *not* pursuing such a course.

Nearly 10 years into our effort, there is compelling evidence to support the benefit. Of course, now there are others with a Kaizen process, and black-belt training, and the many other initiatives you will read about, which are simply other ways to intensify the focus and create further stimulation of ideas.

The Idea Generator was developed by two leading authorities who have helped companies throughout the world stimulate their people to participate more fully in the total improvement process. I trust you will enjoy learning and reading about Quick and Easy Kaizen, as I have. And I hope you will also benefit by hearing from some of Dana's managers as they relate their successful methods for stimulating creative thought and positive results.

Sincerely,

Joe Magliochetti
Chairman - CEO
Dana Corporation

Table of Contents

The Idea Generator

Quick and Easy Kaizen

Change

Creativity

Involvement

Empowerment

The goal of this book is to guide improvement activities throughout the organization: to use creative ideas from all employees to serve both internal and external customers, to unlock the hidden potential of every single employee, and to bring new excitement and joy into the workplace.

Bunji Tozawa

Norman Bodek

Edited by Shelly Rivoli and Beth Simone

Bunji Tozawa – Norman Bodek

Introduction

I have been to Japan 54 times in the last 24 years, searching for the best management tools I could find—the very techniques that moved Japan from a nation noted for producing "junk" to the second most powerful industrial society in the world. When I first visited Japan I felt like Aladdin from the Arabian Nights, accidentally stumbling into a cave and discovering all those wonderful hidden manufacturing management jewels.

During these ongoing journeys to the East, I met and published the works of many creative management geniuses, including Dr. Shigeo Shingo and Taiichi Ohno, the co-creators and discoverers of the Toyota Production System: Just-In-Time (JIT) Lean Management. In fact, on each of these trips another jewel would serendipitously reveal itself. I discovered and published works on:

> Customer Service
> Benchmarking
> Cause & Effect Diagram with the addition of cards
>   (CEDAC)
> Cost Management and Management Accounting
> Hoshin Kanri – Quality policy deployment system
> Kaizen Teian
> The New Standardization
> One Piece Flow & Kanban key elements to JIT
> Poka-Yoke – Misproofing techniques
> Quality Function Deployment (QFD)
> The Seven New QC Tools
> Single Minute Exchange of Die (SMED)
> Total Productive Maintenance (TPM)
> Total Quality Control (TQC)

Total Quality Management (TQM)
Variety Reduction Planning (VRP)
Visual Factory and 5S – Visual management techniques

On 35 of my trips to Japan, I lead groups of senior executives and managers on industrial study missions, visiting over 250 offices and factories in search of new ideas that could improve productivity, quality, and customer service.

As a result, JIT and the other management concepts we discovered have proven invaluable to American industry. This information has allowed American companies to become much more competitive in the global market. JIT has revolutionized manufacturing and, in terms of dollar benefits, is the leading concept discovered on those trips. JIT focuses on reducing the timeline to deliver products and services by eliminating all the non-value adding wastes. However, we've found that JIT neglects to answer important questions about how to involve and motivate people in their personal quest for self-satisfaction at work.

In the past, companies with great innovative leaders could move and motivate thousands to succeed; but in this 21st century, it takes the coordinated spirit and energies of all employees. It might once have been possible for just a few leaders to solve many of a company's problems, but today the world is so highly competitive, and is made so much smaller by the Internet, jet transport, satellite communications, and other advanced technologies, that we need everyone's brainpower. We need everyone in our organization to be involved in improvement activities. Today we want every employee to fully participate in solving problems and finding new solutions.

The Idea Generator – Quick and Easy Kaizen

One "jewel" I discovered during my travels did relate to motivating and involving employees: Kaizen Teian. I remember visiting Toyota and Canon, where both were receiving over 60 to 70 improvement ideas in writing per employee per year—compared to less than one in America at that time. Unfortunately, the executives who were traveling on these trips thought that this system was merely a game, unique to Japan, created simply to keep the workers happy. As I observed these companies and their employees first-hand, I felt strongly that it was much more. But, since I was not an industrial engineer or a manufacturing manager, I was unable to stimulate greater interest in Kaizen except with a few companies. Dana Corporation, as you will see in this book, was one of the exceptions.

On each study mission to Japan I would include special visits to offices and manufacturing plants to see the Kaizen system in action. I would ask our Japanese management guides to point out some of the ideas installed by the workers. When approached, you could see the workers bubbling with pride as each showed us something that he or she had personally accomplished.

I was also intrigued when I saw that both workers on the factory floor, in the office, in stores and hospitals were coming up with small ideas to improve their own work. I immediately searched for Japanese books on the subject, and I was so fortunate to meet Bunji Tozawa, a consultant, a teacher, the author of 21 books on Kaizen, and now the CEO of the HR Association in Japan.

Bunji Tozawa leads the effort to open up the infinite creative potential locked within each worker. It's not unlike discovering the power locked inside an atom. Who in the past would have believed that the tiny atom could have such hidden power? Yet, when released, that energy can have an enormous effect. Similarly, how many managers still look at their employees as "drones, unable to find creative ideas?" Yet, locked inside every individual is the infinite creative capacity for change. And just as **it took forward-thinking scientists to unlock the power in the atom, it takes enlightened management to unlock the creative potential of all of their employees.**

In truth, people have lots of very good ideas on how to improve their own work. The problem is that they are hardly ever asked for their ideas, and most companies do not have a system to encourage their employees to develop, install, manage, and sustain those ideas. But Kaizen Teian seemed to be doing just that.

I became totally fascinated with the Kaizen system and eventually published five of Tozawa's books in English. With each of these projects, I became more convinced that creativity is the only means by which workers can truly be involved in their company's success.

Nevertheless, Kaizen Teian still was not being utilized in the West. While we picked up JIT, TPM, and most of the other Japanese management techniques, very few American companies adopted Kaizen Teian. I couldn't understand the resistance to this simple but powerful concept of gathering many small improvement ideas from all of the workers. Why wasn't Kaizen Teian being installed in America?

I think I now know the answer.

Kaizen Teian was a suggestion system. And since most suggestion systems are based on ideas for *other* people to do something, not the originator of the suggestion, it is difficult to administer these changes, and the very system can become burdensome to management. However, a suggestion system can have a valuable place in your company if managed exceptionally well.[*]

But Mr. Tozawa and many managers at Japanese companies evolved Kaizen Teian to something new and exciting that seemed to bring a new level of respect to workers in factories, offices, restaurants, hotels, hospitals, and other institutions throughout Japan.

It is called Quick and Easy Kaizen. Quick and Easy Kaizen is a simple but powerful system designed to inspire all employees to generate or offer new improvement ideas on a continuous basis. It enables them to make their own jobs easier, and to take the initiative to make small changes that will help satisfy customers, reduce costs, improve quality and safety, and also to reduce the time it takes to deliver products and services to your customers. Kaizen is a way to get all employees truly involved, fully participating, in identifying and being part of the problem solving process. Most importantly, it focuses on implementing ideas, not on suggesting ideas for others to do something.

There are many books available on how to get innovative ideas to design and sell new products, but there are very few books written on how to stimulate creativity from every employee in the organization. In fact, I recently checked the Amazon.com database and found 2,242 books with the word "Idea" in the title. Why so many books talking about ideas—and why such a large market for these books? Possibly it represents our society's inherent knowledge that we either grow or we wilt. I think this is true of all nature, and is especially true for human beings. To live, our only choice is to grow. And real growth and progress only come from

---

[*] See the Dana Corporation interviews in Part IV of this book.

the generation of new ideas. It is a form of evolution, each of us continually striving for a higher, finer place.

Quick and Easy Kaizen recognizes that every single employee has that creative potential not just a limited few. Quick and Easy Kaizen is the most efficient system I know that encourages people to become responsible for their company's success, and at the same time encourages people to grow personally on the job. It is simple, dynamic, and its effects are immediate. If it is so simple, you might wonder why it hasn't been done before? We've certainly wondered that ourselves! Perhaps this kind of system wasn't implemented sooner because, in the past, management often didn't trust the intelligence of the average worker. If this thinking was ever justified in the past, it certainly isn't today. Just call a Dana manager and ask what he thinks of his people's ability to come up with simple but important improvement ideas? I did call a number of Dana managers after they implemented this kind of system and listened to their excitement. You can find their interviews in Part IV of this book.

The purpose of this book is to teach you how to encourage and support others to come up with small improvement ideas on a regular and sustained basis, ideas that can be self-installed on the job to make work easier, to give a sense of achievement and also add to the overall success of the company. It is written for managers and executives, leaders in the workplace, and for those interested in improving their own work lives by helping to make work more interesting, more enjoyable, and fun.

The Idea Generator – Quick and Easy Kaizen

Let's make our work enjoyable and fun!

It is especially designed for those who are in a position to promote improvement in the workplace. In the following pages, we will define and explain the:

- 3 definitions of Kaizen
- 3 rules of Kaizen
- 3 elements that make a Kaizen system work well
- 3 stages of how to develop your own Kaizen system
- 3 principles to apply
- 3 essential steps of Kaizen
- 3 points in a Kaizen report – memo
- 3 obstacles or blocks to a creative idea system
- 3 reasons to have a Quick and Easy Kaizen system
- Plus much more to help make your system work and work well.

You might use this book to strengthen your team activities, or to challenge everyone in your company to come up with new and fresh ideas to help solve problems—or just to improve the workplace in general. Our prime focus here is to help you generate lots of improvement ideas from all employees, and empower them to install their own ideas.

We hope to inspire you to start a new improvement process within your organization that will generate thousands of improvement ideas to make your work environment more productive, offer higher quality products and services, to improve safety, to reduce costs and to improve customer service.

Just imagine the impact of thousands of improvement ideas to make your work environment more productive, to offer higher quality products and services, to improve safety, to reduce costs and to improve customer service. Once you start asking for ideas from all employees, and support and encourage those ideas to continuously come to the surface, you will be amazed at the benefits to the employees and the results for the organization. You will find that Quick and Easy Kaizen is truly an Idea Generator.

Everyone is Unhappy in Company A

We want everyone happy like in Company B, using Quick and Easy Kaizen

It is also our hope that this book will bring a greater appreciation of the Kaizen method to American managers. If the United States is to continue its leadership role and sustain its economic strength, it must tap into the hidden wealth and treasures locked away inside each of its working people.

Like Aladdin, I urge you to look around and begin to find the treasures locked inside every single one of your employees. Bring out those hidden jewels and you will be amazed.

Norman Bodek

(This book started from the writings of Bunji Tozawa translated from Japanese to English. I then developed the material, added my experiences with Kaizen these past twenty years and share many of my stories shown throughout the book in italics.)

Part I

What is Kaizen?
Definitions, Structure, and Systems

Part I Overview

*"The never-ending task of
self improvement . . ."*
Ralph Waldo Emerson

Most people familiar with Asian management methods already know that Kaizen is a Japanese word meaning continuous improvement. They would agree that it means **creating an atmosphere of continuous improvement by changing your view, changing your method, and your way of thinking to make something better or for something to become better.** However, if you ask a number of different people to give you their own definitions of Kaizen, the answers you receive will likely be as varied and numerous as the people you ask. In other words, there are many different—and acceptable—definitions of Kaizen.

Some say that because Kaizen means change, it emphasizes innovation. And while some would argue that Kaizen is about making changes on a large scale, others believe Kaizen encourages small and simple changes. In some sense, all of these people are right. Let us explain.

Kaizen is an improvement process that has evolved substantially over the years. As a result, the term Kaizen has developed to have multiple meanings. There is the Kaizen Blitz technique, which is a training system that brings work teams together onto the factory floor to make improvements, to move machines and reduce the cycle time. There is also Kaizen Teian, the more traditional suggestion system.

The Idea Generator – Quick and Easy Kaizen

The version we teach in this book is different from both of these methods of Kaizen and, with a few exceptions, is quite different from anything taught in America before. Therefore, to teach Quick and Easy Kaizen, we must first explain what we mean when we use the term 'Kaizen'.

For our purposes, the **3 definitions of Kaizen** are:

1. Improvement through changes in the method
2. Small changes, not big changes
3. Changes within realistic constraints

Of course, it's possible to talk about Kaizen in a more elaborate manner, adding numerous definitions, and discussing more of its history in detail. But, experience has taught us that's not necessary. Kaizen is, by it's nature, simple.

In the next few chapters we will illustrate how each of these definitions is critical to the success of Kaizen. But first, let us introduce you to the best way we've found yet to turn ideas into success.

---

3 Definitions of Kaizen

1. **Change the method**
2. **Small changes**
3. **Changes within realistic constraints**

Chapter 1: Turning Ideas into Success

"Ask your employees the question,
'If you owned this company what
would you do to improve it?'"
Jack Simms

There are some questions frequently asked by most managers:

- How do I motivate my employees?
- How do I get my employees to become more involved and take more ownership of their jobs?
- How can my employees better serve our internal and external customers?
- How can I help people feel personally responsible for our company's success?
- How do I get my employees excited about their work?
- How do I get my employees involved in improvement activities?
- How can I foster and administer change activities?
- How can I lead my employees to bring positive change to the organization?

These are very important questions, and Quick and Easy Kaizen can help you answer all of them. Quick and Easy Kaizen is a very simple but powerful methodology to encourage and manage change within the workplace, change that will stimulate employees to become more motivated, more excited, more involved—and ultimately to feel better about themselves and the companies they work for.

In this book, we will examine each of these questions and explain directly what Quick and Easy Kaizen is about. Moreover, we will give you the necessary tools and techniques to enhance change activities for your employees, to strengthen your company's competitive position, to better serve your customers, and to aid you in your personal growth.

As a manager, supervisor, or engineer, you already know there is nothing more rewarding than to get people excited about their work. If you want to learn powerful ways of motivating your employees—to better serve their customers and improve their own lives at work—please read on.

Challenge all employees to be responsible for change!

Quick and Easy Kaizen is a system for employees to turn their own ideas into the success of the company—and themselves. It gives them a tremendous sense of pride and accomplishment in their own work, and it encourages workers to install changes that will please their internal and external customers.[**] The collective result of installing so many ideas brings new energy to the work place and helps employees feel directly responsible for the company's financial success and the competitiveness of their organization.

---

[*] An internal customer is the next person using your work, while the external customer is the one who ultimately pays for your product or service.

The Idea Generator – Quick and Easy Kaizen

Unlike many other improvement methods, Quick and Easy Kaizen is not a typical "suggestion system." Workers do not present their ideas and wait for someone else to implement them. Quick and Easy Kaizen is a system of encouraging employees to come up with small ideas and implement the ideas themselves. It is an important system that helps all employees recognize their infinite creative potential and become more involved in the improvement process within their company.

We are sure that you know the value of getting people involved; therefore, it's essential that you engage your employees in meaningful improvement activities. According to Cambridge's International Dictionary of English, engage is defined as follows:

engage, *v.t.*, to cause (someone) to be interested in something and to keep thinking about it, or to attract and keep (someone's interest)

Isn't that exactly what you want?

People can make a difference at the work place!

Once again, let us make perfectly clear that we are not talking about suggestions for other people. Rather, we are talking about a system that helps people take ownership of their work as they install their own improvement ideas.

Quick and Easy Kaizen is a simple and effective way to inspire this kind of thinking in your employees and encourage them to experiment—to experience the fun and satisfaction of coming up with a new idea that can solve a problem, to implement a solution and write up the idea to display and share with others.

Quick and Easy Kaizen encourages people to come up with small ideas to change their jobs for the better. And when you implement each employee's ideas for improvement across the company, you will begin to see a total transformation take place. You will see happier people, vast improvement in people's attitudes about themselves, productivity and quality will improve, safety will improve, costs will go down, and your customers will be more satisfied. They all go together as people become more focused, more involved, in making their work easier and improving the work environment.

**When people discover an improvement idea and install it,
it is just like finding gold!**

Small changes add up to major improvements!

JIT, TPM, TQM and the other management systems have proven beneficial in making industry more efficient and effective. But these new systems have only had a marginal effect on improving the quality of work life for individual workers.

Instead of asking managers to find new ways to enrich people's work lives, Quick and Easy Kaizen shifts the responsibility to the worker. The employees are told to come up with small, simple ideas on a regular basis. For each new idea, an employee will:

The Idea Generator – Quick and Easy Kaizen

- **Present an idea to her supervisor,**
- **Keep the supervisor informed of her daily progress,**
- **Write up the idea to share with co-workers, and**
- **Report back on her successes or needs for additional assistance.**

Following are two examples of Quick and Easy Kaizen memos from Dana Corporation[*]:

Exhibit 1-1 Reducing the expense of mailing

Before improvement	After improvement
High expense of mailing W2 forms	W2 forms sorted by department
Effect: W2 forms now distributed at the plant instead of being mailed	
Submitted By: Kathy	

Exhibit 1-2 Prevention of oil mist over operator

Before improvement	After improvement
Oil mist over ID grinder operator	Moved the wall near the ID grinder
Effect: To keep the oil mist off the operator	
Submitted By: Elton	

What a wonderful way to please your internal customer!

These are very small ideas, but imagine how the employee feels when his ideas are accepted and installed?

---

[*] The utilization and formation of Quick and Easy Kaizen memo will be explained in Part II, Chapter 7.

In Portland, Oregon, one worker at the JAE Corporation submitted an idea: "Turn off the lights." A very simple idea, but that simple idea saved the company $6,000 last year! Of course, this idea may seem rather obvious, but too often it's the obvious that is neglected.

Turn off the lights

Kaizen begins with you!

To recap, a successful Kaizen system includes all employees, company-wide, in continuous improvements that make their jobs easier, improve the work process and satisfy their customers. For a Kaizen system to operate smoothly, each employee must meet the following conditions:

- **To quickly and easily write down an idea.**
- **To quickly and easily implement it.**

Once we have sufficient practice in implementing and documenting Kaizen (small changes), we can ingrain the process and make it a habit—a good habit! While studying this book and putting the concepts into practice, please continue to focus on these two points.

Also, as you read this book, jot down on a separate piece of paper (or in the back of the book) any improvement ideas that you've had for your own job, or perhaps for someone else's. If you think of any ideas you've had and already implemented, jot down what the problem was, your solution, and the subsequent effect. And if you can think of any problems that you're currently faced with at work, but have not yet come up with solutions for, be sure to jot those down too. Jot away!

As you continue to read you will have several opportunities to write down Kaizen examples as exercises. We want to help you see for yourself that you can document improvements quickly and easily. After all, Quick and Easy Kaizen asks every employee to become responsible for improving his own work—and for making that work easier, more interesting, and more pleasing to his customers. But don't forget, this means you too!

Not long ago, a client of mine who is a senior executive at a very large chain store called me and said, "Norm, how can we educate and train over 100,000 employees to improve customer service? We want a totally new image in the marketplace. We want to be known as the best chain store in America. But how is it possible to move, to motivate, to change the behavior of 100,000 employees who are used to their old ways of doing things?" That is a very good question. How can you motivate people to change their old ways of doing things? Instead of directing those 100,000 people to change their behavior, it is far easier to ask them for their help and their ideas, and to give them a new system where their ideas are not only heard but are rapidly implemented, and to their credit.

I did visit some of their stores and met many people, with hope, that management would begin to bring positive change to the company. I asked some of them to offer suggestions on how they would improve customer service. A few were completely distrustful of me and offered nothing, but one exceptionally grateful person was so appreciative to have someone that honestly wanted her opinion. She said, "In all my 18 years working for this store, no one has ever asked me that question." Imagine that! She had many ideas to offer. And to demonstrate to me, she noticed a customer waiting at the check out counter and went over and opened a new cash register just so that customer would not have to wait on line.

I recommended that the chain store immediately train people on Quick and Easy Kaizen and begin to listen to them. Believe me the average employee has multitude of ideas on how to bring improvements, just install a system that asks them for their ideas and lets them install them on their own.

Summary

Quick and Easy Kaizen...

1. **is an improvement system that includes ALL EMPLOYEES**

2. **shifts the responsibility for improvement to the worker**

3. **focuses on small changes that can be applied immediately**

4. **requires each person to write down and implement his own ideas**

5. **begins with you!**

Chapter 2: Improving by Changing Methods

*"First, have a definite, clear practical ideal;
a goal, an objective. Second, have the
necessary means to achieve your ends;
wisdom, money, materials, and methods.
Third, adjust all your means to that end."*

Aristotle

Improve by changing methods with a truly positive spirit

We would like to use the word "shortcut" from here on out to mean improvement. But we must be careful using the English word shortcut, for it does have many connotations!

When we say that Kaizen is a shortcut, some people might say, "That's out of the question! Shortcut?" They might argue this point. Of course, if we are talking about simple shortcuts without consideration of the results then we can expect to have accidents or the quality of our services might be reduced. But we are talking about making small improvements that will make the work easier to do.

For our purposes, "shortcut" means:

I.   **A route that is shorter or more direct than the usual one.**

II.   **A way of saving time and effort in doing something.**

However, a Kaizen shortcut isn't cutting corners. It isn't doing things foolishly or without thought, and it certainly doesn't mean that we will jeopardize the process or be careless in attaining our goals.

Many companies, of course, do improvement activities. In a nutshell, we are asking you to promote improvement activities among your employees that involve making shortcuts—doing their same jobs more quickly or more easily, and in fewer steps.

> **Ask your employees to find a new way to do things more quickly, or skip doing unnecessary things. That is Kaizen activity.**

The reason many companies establish a Kaizen system and run Kaizen seminars is to promote a system that finds ways to involve all workers to make improvements, and to do it with a truly positive spirit—whereby people are happier with their work, themselves, and their associates.

Since people are not always looking for possible shortcuts, their work often doesn't go smoothly and problems can occur. And when workers are not striving to change and improve their methods, they often become bored with their work.

"No fun, no fun, no fun at all"

The Idea Generator – Quick and Easy Kaizen

We want workers to make improvements and find shortcuts, but with the right spirit. We do not want to coerce or force the worker to make improvements. We want them to understand how they and the company benefit together from their improvement efforts. It will bring them new energy into their workday.

"They really liked my idea."

"Doing shortcuts seriously" is the meaning of Kaizen activity. **You should be asking each employee to find a new way to shortcut or skip doing unnecessary things.** In fact, you start Quick and Easy Kaizen by asking everyone in the company to come up with two improvement ideas in writing every month. Then you give them training and show some examples on how it works. Once that's done, you simply listen and support the efforts of your employees—and watch as your workplace brims with new energy and enthusiasm.

Simple!

One of my favorite examples of a shortcut comes from a visit I made to a Canon camera factory. Near an operator was a simple bucket, but this one had wheels on it. This operator came up with the idea to put wheels on the bucket so that when she finished her assembly work, without getting up, she would place her completed parts into the bucket and just kick the bucket forward to the next operator. The next operator would take out the parts and kick the bucket back to the previous operator. A very simple and very effective shortcut.

Shortcut by changing methods

Kaizen is a shortcut whereby you change the method responsibly; if the shortcut is not backed by a change in the methods, we cannot call that Kaizen. And if we do not change the method, then people have a tendency to go back to the "same old ways of doing things."

Say you have a habit of putting papers to be filed into a pile, off in the corner of your office. Naturally, you intend to file these papers—eventually; you just don't consider filing a value-adding process, so it takes the back burner. But once in a while when you feel inspired and get tired of looking at the pile, you take the time to file the papers away. Here's the difference: If you file the papers away, but begin a new pile the very next day, your filing is not a Kaizen activity—you have not changed the method! But if you create a new method whereby you file the papers either immediately, or at least at the end of each day, then you are doing Kaizen.

Simply put, **Kaizen is changing the method and/or the ingenuity of the means for improvement. But a shortcut without changing methods could be called simple negligence.** It could cause unfavorable situations like more accidents, more defects, poor service, and fewer sales. That's why one of the most important things to remember about implementing new shortcuts is that

when we change the method we don't go back to the "old way of doing things."

Exhibit 2-1 and 2-2 are the examples of shortcut by changing methods at Dana Corporation.

Exhibit 2-1 Change the routing form distribution method

Before improvement:	After improvement:
Couldn't always find the driver to give him his routing forms	Made an in-out box in the cast iron room to place the routing forms
Effect: Time saved, no need to look for the driver any time to give him routing forms. **Submitted By**: James	

Exhibit 2-2 Change the path of leaked oil

Before improvement:	After improvement:
Index box leaked oil on the floor	Removed drain plug and replaced it with a nipple and drain hose to waste oil jug
Effect: No longer have to drain the index box or clean up the floor. **Submitted By**: James	

Basically, the more shortcuts you can discover, the more chances you have to do a better job. Through conscious Kaizen activity, we can find shortcuts to eliminate many unnecessary tasks that do not add value to our products and services. Without short-cuts, the tendency is to omit or even cut back on doing important things. The excess time gained through shortcuts can be invested on important and absolutely necessary things for work, which we cannot omit.

Selecting Alternative Means or Changing the Methods to Achieve Better Objectives

*"I cannot teach anybody anything,
I can only make them think."*
Socrates

Make productivity and service improvements by changing the methods

So far, we've talked about the first definition of Kaizen meaning to make improvements or make shortcuts. (For those people who still have difficulty in accepting the word "shortcut," we recommend you use another word that you are more comfortable with, so long as it means finding a better way or changing methods.) Now we will discuss how these shortcuts can be made to last.

Each person's job has objectives, including the task itself, responsibility for the outcome, and so forth. This is true whether they are making something, transporting something, or selling something. And these objectives must be accomplished because, in exchange for fulfilling those objectives, they are earning a living. If we don't accomplish that, the objectives of our jobs, we may be fired or receive a reduced wage or salary, or maybe we will be transferred to somewhere else.

However, there are often many different methods or means to accomplish job objectives. **If there is only one method to accomplish that objective, of course we don't need to improve—** there is no room for improvement! And the only thing we need to do is follow the old method, day in and day out.

31

As you review Kaizen examples scattered throughout this book, you can see many means and methods to accomplish an objective. When we say that Kaizen means changing methods, we mean that when we make improvements we do not go back to the old ways of doing things. Again, just cleaning up is not Kaizen if the system allows us to begin cluttering again.

A problem I once noticed in a store was that many boxes were being piled one on top of another, even though only a few boxes were required at the time. To prevent over ordering and reduce the inventory, a bar was placed on the floor, which restricted the number of boxes that could be piled on top of each other – that bar was Kaizen.

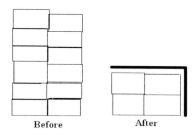

Before   After

The iron bar is a method to reduce inventory

Exhibit 2-3 Reducing unnecessary inventory

Before improvement:	After improvement:
Order of parts too high	Cancelled 600 piece part, reset the standard order to only 10 pieces.
Effect: Reduced inventory and saved $10,842.00 **Submitted By**: Phoebe	

The Idea Generator – Quick and Easy Kaizen

The bar was a method that did not allow you to go back to the old ways of doing things. And as you can see by the report, this simple Kaizen proved to be an effective improvement.

Many people, however, have a tendency to stick to only one method they have learned. They have been told to do something in a certain way or they have a method that has been successful in the past. They tend to stick to those methods.

However, in reality, the environment of how we have to do our job has been changing rapidly. Methods necessary in the past have no guarantee that we will need to do that now. The method that was good in the past may not be useful these days. In the worst case, maybe it becomes an obstacle to accomplishing the new objective. **Therefore, the best method yesterday may not be the best today**.

We need to change according to the changes in our surroundings and we should change our methods by selecting the best way to do things. Kaizen means selecting the better way to do things and to change our methods accordingly. We don't have to stick to the way one person has continually done it, or to the historical methods. We need to think of different ways, we need to study different methods and think about it and devise new ways of doing things.

Kaizen means:

I. Selecting a better way to do things
II. Don't stick to just one way or the old way
III. Think, study, and devise new ways to do things

When I moved to Portland, Oregon around ten years ago, I found a Safeway Supermarket near my house. When I first entered the store my initial impressions were very negative. "This is not a store where I would buy my food and supplies," I said. The store was dirty, in disarray, and unappealing.

Well, four years later while I was running a seminar on customer service, I asked the seminar attendees to tell us, "Who delivers great customer service?" One person said, "Safeway." I was so surprised. The very next day I went and visited a Safeway store to see what had happened to cause such a positive reaction.

It was true. Safeway had completely changed. The floors sparkled, shelves and boxes were superbly displayed and aligned, and I was greeted with a smile and a "Good morning," and at the check out counter I was told, "Thank you Mr. Bodek for shopping with us today." Safeway had changed their method. Everyone who worked at Safeway now smiles, greets the customer, makes eye contact, takes the customer to the aisle, lets the customer taste the product, mentions the customer's name at the check out counter, and actually treats all customers just the way you would greet a guest in your home.

Safeway's new method to greet their customers

Step	Actions
1	Greet each customer with a smile
2	Anticipate needs
3	You take the customer to the item
4	Let customer sample products and you make suggestions
5	Thank the customer by last name
6	Offer carry-out service
7	Offer a parting comment, invite them back

It's simple but very powerful when you measure these every week. Mystery shoppers each week inspect. The managers and all of the employees know how well they are doing in greeting and treating their customers like guests. Last year, Safeway was given the highest rating in customer service by a local newspaper survey in Vancouver, Washington, where I now live and work. So simple! They changed their method and, in four years, went from probably the worst supermarket chain to the best and all they did was simply change their methods of greeting and treating their customers as guests.

Shortcuts with a purpose

We can also say Kaizen is making "shortcuts with a purpose," or with objectives. We are not encouraging you to do shortcuts without any objective or purpose! The goal here is to come up with a shortcut to fulfill your existing job objectives or to improve those objectives.

In a nutshell, Kaizen means priority thinking, learning how to prioritize everything we do, and trying to single out the most important things. We want you to focus on what you consider to be the most important things to be done, and this training book will help you identify what those things are.

Of course, if we don't understand our job objectives clearly, we cannot come up with a shortcut with a purpose. People who don't understand their job objectives tend to say, "We are told to do this. We are supposed to be doing this" and so forth, even if it doesn't make sense. This is not Kaizen!

In order for change to truly improve the work, we must **shortcut with responsibility**. We are not encouraging people to implement shortcuts irresponsibly. The shortcut has to fulfill the job responsibly. And how much responsibility a worker can take for a shortcut must be proportionate to the individual's ability, experience, and position.

Try it!

List some ideas that could help you shortcut or skip doing unnecessary tasks in your own job. We'll come back to these ideas in a later chapter.

_____

_____

_____

_____

The Idea Generator – Quick and Easy Kaizen

Summary

Kaizen is a shortcut...

1. with a purpose
2. with objective consciousness
3. that better accomplishes job objectives
4. that changes methods
5. made with responsibility

Chapter 3: Small Changes, Not Big Changes

"We are always looking for small incremental improvements. We always want to challenge the status quo."

**Bryan Bergsteinsson,
Lexus group vice president
and general manager**

Of course, we want all of the best ideas to be implemented, but to make a Quick and Easy Kaizen system work well we focus only on small changes not big changes, but small changes that can be done quickly, easily, and continuously

Management normally looks for the big ideas that can be meaningful. But very few employees can find and make big improvements. So when you focus on big ideas people just stop and do not offer the small ideas that collectively are very powerful. Quick and Easy Kaizen is a system to get all employees involved in making improvements on a continuous basis, to do that we focus only on small changes.

This is one of the most common misunderstandings about Kaizen. Too often we hear people say that changing the method of work is too much or too difficult to do. There are people involved with ISO 9000 or ISO 14000 who are fearful of letting people make changes that might affect their standards. But **Quick and Easy Kaizen is small changes, and these small changes very rarely affect the standards.**

But try as we may, there are still people who continue to think that Kaizen is only big changes. It is difficult to convince them differently even though we show them many successful cases and talk about Kaizen being simple. They tend to say, "Well, if we let people be involved in making changes then we have to continuously change the standards and we will lose control."

Believe us, you will not lose control. First, very few of the small Kaizen ideas will affect your standards. And second, if an improvement idea from an employee does reduce costs, improve quality or safety, the supervisor will decide if the installation of the idea is worth the time and effort to change the standard. To be competitive, organizations must continuously improve, and standards should keep up with those improvements. **Quick and Easy Kaizen focuses only on small changes and encourages all employees to be involved in improvement activities.**

However, as we have already mentioned, our use of the word Kaizen does not mean "big changes." Think of **Kaizen as an accumulation of small changes, little by little.**

Exhibit 3-1 Changing a small part reduced set up time

Before improvement:	After improvement:
Part number 250768 used a different nose at turn causing much set-up time	Modified locator so we could use a quick-change nose plate
Effect: Reduced set-up time **Submitted By**: Ray	

Exhibit 3-2 Small change for a safer working environment

Before improvement:	After improvement:
Broken skid on the floor	Removed the busted skid
Effect: Prevent possible accident of people from tripping over the skid	
Submitted By: Charles	

I recently visited around a dozen supermarkets and drug stores. I would see packages, boxes piled in the aisles, paper scattered on the floor, shelves with merchandise in disarray, floors and ceilings with torn tiles, window fronts with junk piled up. It just looked as if all the managers and employees of the store came to work every day without anyone stopping to look with fresh eyes at their surroundings. If we just stop, take a deep breath, and look around we can find much to improve.

In fact, I recommend that you take a camera with you to work and take pictures of your work areas.

Share those pictures with your fellow workers and do Kaizen, find ways to improve the method so that the work place looks appealing to both employees and guests. Take pictures again a month later of the same area. Then simply hang up the picture where all can see the before and after pictures. Repeat this process for a few months and you will be amazed at the changes that will take place.

Doing Kaizen also helps people to be more alert to potential dangers. Kaizen means changing the way you do your job, but the degree of change could be big, moderate or small. There are different scales. If you are aiming to change the way you are doing your job, or the work method, all at once, that is more like innovation, renewal, or remodeling. And, of course, with that type of change you can expect a big effect. However, this type of change normally cannot be done easily. It requires lots of investment in time and money and requires special abilities, special technology, and so forth. If it doesn't work, if it fails, the result is also very serious.

Of course, these big changes have to be done in the company, especially by the top management executives. They must fulfill their responsibility to do their management innovation and so forth. That type of innovation is necessary at difficult times, and will be further discussed later in this chapter.

**A big change is not always effective, for
sometimes you miss your target.**

The Idea Generator – Quick and Easy Kaizen

**A big change becomes effective when it is complemented
by small changes (like small jabs followed by a big hit).**

At the end of World War II, America was the strongest, richest, most productive and innovative country in the world. During the 1950s enormous new technologies helped to surge our country's productivity growth. During the 1960s we wasted much of our economic advantages in the war in Vietnam and we became complacent and our productivity growth started to decline. Like the story of the tortoise and the hare we rested on our laurels.

Kaizen is small changes

While we rested in the United States, the Japanese focused on the reconstruction of their industries, using the United States as a model. Slowly, like the tortoise in the story, Japan's industry improved continuously, with their productivity and the quality of their products improving at a much faster rate than ours.

It was during this time that Japanese companies established Kaizen and other improvement activities to inch closer and closer to us. They involved all employees in improvement activities, both individually and in teams.

Luckily, the US woke up again in the mid-to-late 1980s to create new technologies that would boost our productivity, and the US lead the world in wealth and prosperity once again. But American companies should not become complacent again; they should simply continue to innovate and to continuously improve. Quick and Easy Kaizen ensures that everyone in your company will participate in the improvement activities.

Please note, there are American companies that have already implemented Quick and Easy Kaizen. In this book we often refer to the success of the Dana Corporation, which is gathering millions of implemented ideas from all of its employees.

Kaizen is Quickly, Simply, Easily, Persistently, Tenaciously, and Continuously Sustained and Repeated

Instead of always telling people what to do, it is far better to ask them questions, provide a little guidance and let them discover solutions on their own.

Kaizen is involving all employees on a day-to-day basis, continuously

In 'Quick & Easy Kaizen' we are looking for small, constant improvements. Most people look to make big 'meaningful' changes, something they can 'write home about.' But usually there is tremendous resistance to making big changes. As well, there is danger in making big changes, for big changes can lead to big problems. If you make a big mistake it can be very costly and might be difficult to correct, but if you make a small mistake you can easily make a correction.

Again, we are not talking about large-scale changes. Kaizen means small-scale changes, made little by little. That is Kaizen. For large-scale changes, we use another word: "innovation."

When a big change or innovation fails, the result is also big. Therefore, big changes have to be done prudently and should be part of your long-term planning, not a part of your Kaizen activities.

When I started to write the 'Quick & Easy Kaizen' book, I said I have to practice what I preach, so I looked around my office area and noticed in front of me at least a year's worth of needed improvements. I took many pictures of my work area to represent the 'Before Improvement.'

One area neglected was the area just behind my desk. As I added computer equipment, the cables behind my desk would just pile up. And when I needed to get to a file cabinet I would invariably trip, pulling out a cable and causing some electrical problem.

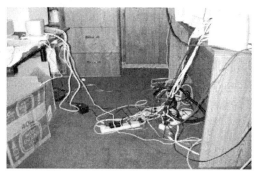

Before Improvement.

After first improvement step.

The Idea Generator – Quick and Easy Kaizen

After second improvement step.

Not perfect yet, but getting there.

Now that I am teaching 'Quick & Easy Kaizen,' I try to do Kaizen continuously on my own work and not postpone it. If possible, I want to do a "Kaizen a day."

These are very small steps in my goal to become more efficient. Kaizen is making very small improvements. I have a lot of opportunities to improve my office area, my desk, my in and out basket, my bookshelves, my filing system, my "to-do" list, etc. If you came in to my office today, I would be quite embarrassed at the mess, but if you come in a few months, I'm hoping I'll be proud to show you around!

Kaizen is continuous trial and error, within the scope of your own job

Since we are talking about small changes, we recommend they be done quickly and easily. If the Kaizen you try doesn't work, you should improve on it. **Kaizen allows for continuous trial and error.** The reason is that the boundary of Kaizen is determined by each individual's experience, position and capabilities.

In other words, the boundary of Kaizen for each person must be within the scope of his job and capabilities. If the changes are beyond his capabilities, he shouldn't tackle it quickly or easily! However, if it is within the framework, and that person can do it, then the Kaizen can and should be done in a more relaxed manner—simply, quickly, and easily. Even if it is a small Kaizen, when you complete it you can feel good about your accomplishment and reap the benefits right away.

I had too many file folders in my computer, so I combined the files to make the list smaller. Instead of searching through many file folders, I made 10 major folders and also set up sub-folders within the major folders. Now on one screen I could quickly see and find the documents I needed to work with. It was such a small Kaizen, but it was a shortcut and cut down my search time. Unfortunately, that little change unexpectedly caused havoc with my Franklin Planner program.

I used the Franklin Planner program to keep all of my addresses and telephone numbers. But, now after moving folders the planner program wouldn't work. I was a little frustrated.

Hold on, there must be a better solution?

I didn't think that just moving folders would cause problems like this. I wanted to call Dell Computer for help, but I had diffi-

culty finding their telephone number, as the number was in my Franklin planner. When I finally found a number and called Dell Computer, I spent the next two hours on the phone trying to discover a solution. However, even after those two hours Dell couldn't help me.

I then called Franklin Covey, waited 21 minutes to be connected, but finally a technician named Mark helped me and, with patience, guided me through several processes that corrected the registry and restored the program, and thankfully all the files were fully recovered.

From this experience, I recognized that even small changes could pose new problems. I did suffer for a few moments. Well, a couple of hours actually! But, temporary problems should not stop us from making changes. Many things that we do are fraught with possible problems, but that is life. We should never use the possibility of problems as an excuse to not make progress.

And the bottom line is, it was worth the pain of a temporary setback. I now find it so much easier to look through my computer file folders! And hopefully, I've learned a useful lesson—I will exercise a little bit more care the next time I make changes like that. It will not prevent me from doing more Kaizens; I will just stop and a study a little longer before I make new changes in the computer.

Kaizen is not a home run. It is a single.

Not only should Kaizen be done quickly and easily, it should be done persistently, tenaciously, and continuously!

In a baseball game, you can score with a single home run. But a Kaizen is not a home-run hit; it is a single. One single by itself is not enough to score. It will take additional hits for you to round the bases and score.

Kaizen activity is the accumulation of continuous hits.

Therefore, the most important aspect of the Kaizen activity is the continuous, sustained activity. Keep playing! The single Kaizen effect may be small, but with continuous accumulated effect it can produce good results.

Many business books use bullish expressions like "completely," "boldly," and often they promote a "complete solution" or "changing from the roots." It all sounds good, too. However, the reality is that these big changes are most often not done in a single stroke. It may look like something big will happen, but very often they talk about the changes only on the surface. And in most successful cases, the actual changes happened slowly and widely. It was not done overnight. Instead, the change was progressing underneath the surface of the organization, with the results surfacing one day.

This is why we need a targeted number of ideas to be submitted per employee per month. If we keep a constant, steady supply of ideas flowing through the company, improvement will be inevitable.

The Idea Generator – Quick and Easy Kaizen

If you get an improvement idea, or a problem pops into your head as you read this book, then just jot your idea down on one of the Kaizen forms found throughout the chapters, like this one here, and at the end of most chapters.

Quick & Easy KAIZEN	
Before Improvement	After Improvement

The Effect:

Date   Name

Kaizen and the Scale of Changes

"The only thing that makes us happy
when we are at work is good ideas."
Mike Nichols, movie director

Make the changes according to the size of the problem. When we say Kaizen means small changes, people inevitably ask the following questions: How does Kaizen relate to quality teams, QC Circles, self-directed work teams, or small group activities? Or which should we do first, Kaizen activities or our team activities? Which should we give priority to? These are the kinds of questions we are asked all the time.

Of course, to answer these questions we have to first look at the kind and size of the problems. In our jobs we have big problems, small problems, and medium-sized problems. For example, say there are big trucks, light pickup trucks or bicycles in a transportation system. If we have a big heavy load to carry, of course, we cannot use a bicycle or even a light pickup truck. On the other hand, if you only need to carry a small item, who wants to charter a large-scale truck?

It's easy to see that, for small problems, a bicycle is handier. You can use it quickly and easily to accomplish the same goal. But a slightly bigger problem will call for a light pickup truck. However, in order to drive the large-scale truck we will need a special license. Similarly, a larger problem-solving situation might require studying quality tools and techniques and so forth before change can be implemented.

Small group activities that involve quality teams, QC Circles, and self-directed work teams are more suitable for medium-size changes. These are the kinds of problems that require more than one person to investigate the problem and all its ramifications.

Medium-size problems often have complications; they normally take time to solve. Therefore, it's not that quick or easy to solve those problems. For medium-size changes or for medium-size problems it is better to use tools and weapons to solve the problems rather than using bare hands. The QC circle members have been taught various QC tools to address these kinds of problems, such as how to collect data and use check sheets; how to brainstorm to gather ideas from all the members of the group; how to chart the data on a graph using the Cause and Effect diagram, the Pareto diagram, the Histogram, the Scatter Diagram, the Control charts, and other statistical tools. All of these can help a group to organize, analyze and discuss the medium-size problem. It is more recommendable for the quality teams to examine and to follow-through certain processes of improvement to determine root causes of these problems and come up with solutions that can be supported by statistics.

Since small changes, on the other hand, are simple and more flexible, we can install them almost as quickly as we think about them. We can write down any number of ideas, and implement one after another. Even if we make a mistake, we can do it over again and make other changes quickly and easily too.

Most importantly, we need to use different methods, different ways of attacking problems according to their size and scope. Therefore **self-directed work teams and Kaizen should be treated differently**.

Scale of changes and corresponding actions

Scale	Action
Large scale changes	**Innovation, 5 to 10 year plan**
Medium sized changes	**Conducting quality control or small group activities**
Small changes	**Doing Quick and Easy Kaizen**

We have to realize that there are times when the individual or the company needs to make big innovative changes. Yet, there will still be a series of small changes continuously building up underneath those big changes, making them possible.

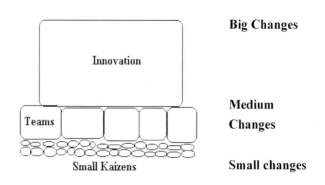

The scale of changes

The Idea Generator – Quick and Easy Kaizen

For example, if you want to change a corporate culture or a company's organizational effectiveness, these types of changes cannot be done overnight. They are the reflections of long-term experience and day-to-day work. It is a reflection based on those accumulated experiences inside the company and the changes made over time.

However, it is these steady, continuous changes that are the essence of Kaizen. And once done, these changes will not allow you to slip back. That is why Kaizen is very steady, safe, and secure change—and that is also how it keeps the workplace energized. Kaizen keeps your energy moving and your ideas flowing as you continuously look for new ways to make your job easier.

Summary

1. **When should you use Quick and Easy Kaizen? When the Kaizen is within the boundaries of your position, experience, and capabilities.**

2. **What if the Kaizen doesn't work? Do Kaizen again. If it still doesn't work, do Kaizen again. If a problem develops from a Kaizen, do another Kaizen until the problem goes away!**

3. **Why should you use Kaizen? To keep the workplace energized and to keep people excited about their jobs.**

Quick & Easy
KAIZEN

Before Improvement	After Improvement

The effect:

Date: **Name:**

Chapter 4: Changes within Realistic Constraints

*"Aim above morality. Be not
simply good, be good for something."*
Henry David Thoreau

Kaizen is to make changes that are practical and within realistic constraints

As we discussed in the previous chapter, Kaizen must be done within the limits established. And it is because we need to work within limitations that we need Kaizen.

Maybe we need more people, or we need more money to solve a problem. Maybe we didn't anticipate all of our future needs and discovered that we don't have the necessary budget in place. **This is the time to be creative.** This is the time to come up with several new Kaizens to help us. For example, say there is a worker who is climbing up and down a ladder, carrying supplies and feeling totally exhausted. He might think of how much better he could work if the company installed an elevator. Instead, he might hook up a temporary pulley to move the material up and down, if that is within the limits of his job.

Why do we need to change the way we do our jobs? Because the limiting conditions of our work have been changing. If there is no change in the condition or situation that we are in, then maybe Kaizen is not necessary. If we were successful in the past and continue to be successful now, then what we all need to do is follow what we have been doing in the same old way as we have been doing it.

However, industry is always changing. Almost every day we can see new materials, new equipment, new technologies, and new ways of doing business, such as the Internet. Technology and systems have been advancing day after day. The systems and regulations within the society have been changing, and deregulation has also affected parts of our industries. Therefore, there are many cases where something that was necessary in the past is no longer necessary at this time. As well, there were times in the past that we couldn't do what we can do now.

If you don't notice any need for changes in the environment you are in, and if you just continue to do your job as you have been doing it in the past, then you shall eventually be in deep trouble. You might begin to see people wasting time unnecessarily, or the workers may get frustrated, or hustle around inefficiently, or maybe they'll begin having trouble dealing with their customers.

You need to review your job and the way you handle your work continually, at a minimum of once a month. Ask yourself these questions:

- **Why do I need to do this?**
- **Why do I need to do this thing to that extent?**

The Idea Generator – Quick and Easy Kaizen

- **Are there any other ways to do this job?**
- **What about other companies, how do they do what I am doing here?**

We each need to review and thoroughly inspect our jobs. That is Kaizen activity.

We want to look closely at what we do

In 1776, when America was born, it took 97% of the people as farmers to feed all 100% of us. In the year 2001, it only takes three out of a 100 to feed us. American farmers have been very productive through continuous improvements, and by continuously being more creative.

Today there are easier ways of doing things

Continuous improvement
involving all employees
through Quick and Easy Kaizen

To maintain our own personal standard of living we must learn, grow, and improve, and for our company to stay competitive it must also be both innovative with new products and services, and it must become more efficient and effective through the creative involvement of all its members. We are in a new millennium, and in this new "information age" everyone must be involved in creative activities to succeed.

As well, it is important that everyone keep the lines of communication open, sharing their ideas with others and reviewing the results together. It is said that it only takes one person to pull the plug and the entire lake goes dry. And it only takes one person to destroy the reliability and integrity of a company. Quick and Easy Kaizen ensures that everyone is aware of the ideas and changes taking place throughout the company.

Years back, the Three Mile Island debacle almost destroyed the entire nuclear power industry because one person knew there was a problem but he also felt that no one would listen to him. So he kept quiet and a whole industry was almost destroyed. There have been more quality disasters and there will continue to be until we learn to listen to the people around us.

Everyone must somehow buy in to the success of their team in order for their team to win. And the best way we've seen to have people buy in is through their own creative ideas, their own creative participation. Kaizen is the key.

Another vital factor is knowing what other, similar companies are doing and achieving, and how they do what we do here. It is vital to examine and look at other companies both in America and throughout the world, and we should especially look outside our own industry.

The Idea Generator – Quick and Easy Kaizen

The first thing we did at Productivity, Inc. in 1981 was to set up a study mission and go see Japan firsthand, to see what the Japanese were doing at the time to have the highest productivity growth rate in the world.

We set up a study mission to Japan through the Japan Productivity Center, in Washington, DC. We advertised in our newsletter and miraculously 19 senior executives signed up to join us on that mission. What we did, as a group, was to participate in one of the first benchmarking trips to Japan. During the process, miracles started to happen. We slowly started to find new and fresh things that the Japanese companies were doing like Just-In-Time production, Total Quality Control (TQC)[*], Quality Circles and Kaizen. Most of us could not believe it when we were told that Toyota and Canon were getting from 60 to 70 ideas in writing per worker per year. Fortunately we had a chance to see many of these small simple ideas installed by workers on the line.

There is a great difference between reading about something and actually seeing it first hand. The old saying, "Seeing is believing," really is true. As we visited the Japanese factories we were very impressed with what we saw. We all returned from that first trip determined that, if the Japanese can do it, so can we!

Benchmarking with the best can add to your strength by giving you the confidence to at least experiment to see if the new ideas would work for your company. I highly recommend that you go to see companies from different industries and that you even visit other countries. It gives you a much wider perspective. If you

---

[*] The name was changed years later to Total Quality Management (TQM)

work for a manufacturing company, go to a Safeway supermarket or Les Schwab's tire store in Portland, Oregon. Go to the Baptist Health System in Pensacola, Florida and see what they did to go from a poorly rated health care provider to the very best in customer satisfaction in just five years. Go to a Dana Corporation plant and talk to their managers about their idea system. You will have fun and learn so much.

Kaizen Activity within very Limited Conditions

"Growth is always met by resistance.
If it is easy to do it then you know
you are not growing."

Rudi

Our work always has limitations, like budget, time, man-power, equipment, facilities, and so forth. Sometimes the limitation is due to human factors or organizational constraints. We might say, "My boss is really stubborn," or "I cannot really rely on my subordinates," and so forth. Everybody works within some kind of constraints.

Therefore, to improve our work through Kaizen, we must be prepared to do it within this environment of restrictions. When we need big changes, but are faced with challenges, we have to break through these restrictions. For example: if we don't have the money, we borrow money from the bank; if we don't have capable employees, we might need to recruit new employees; if we don't have the technology, we buy and introduce new technology; and so forth. Otherwise, we cannot overcome the restrictions and make the big changes.

Kaizen aims for the quick and easy method. Therefore, we don't rely on big changes for overcoming restrictions. If we don't have a large enough budget, we need to come up with ideas that we can do things within our limited budget. If we only have three people to do the job, we need to come up with a method to do the job with three people. That is Kaizen.

63

Please recognize that you might always encounter resistance to new things, but hopefully Quick and Easy Kaizen will help you overcome that resistance and grow. And just think of the wonderful benefits awaiting your employees and the company as a whole.

Not too long ago I was invited to give a presentation on Quick and Easy Kaizen to a group of managers in the Portland area. The managers listened, asked questions and gave me the impression that they liked the idea and saw a need for it in their company. However, their first reaction was to postpone a decision to go ahead and install the system! "Maybe in six months the time would be better to test out the system."

Well, I am sure that in six months, they will find another excuse to postpone making a new decision. I don't mean that disrespectfully; I know that it is very hard to do new things. But if we are to make progress, we simply must test new things. And the time is right. It is right, right now. In this new millennium, with global competition growing, it is vital to gather everyone's ideas to make improvements.

I always remember the words of president Franklin Delano Roosevelt, "the only thing we have to fear is fear itself." Of course we have fears. I remember when I was seven years old I was afraid of swimming over my head. I went to my older brother and asked him to help me to learn how to swim. He did. He picked me up and threw me into deep water and said, "swim." I did. I learned very quickly to overcome my fear. I didn't have much choice. I learned at that moment how to swim.

The Idea Generator – Quick and Easy Kaizen

Some people might say, "you could have drowned," and it was a possibility. But my brother was close by if I did need help. And even though it wasn't exactly what I had in mind when I asked my brother for help... I was still very grateful to have learned to both overcome my fear and to know how to swim.

What to do when change is met with resistance

You will often hear people who are not skilled at Kaizen saying things like, "If we had the money ... if we had the time ... if we had more people," and so forth.

Well, if we have enough money, abundant time, sufficient numbers of skilled people and all the resources we demand for work, then terrific! We don't need Kaizen. But since the vast majority of us have limited funds and time, Kaizen is necessary; we must devise a way to improve our jobs within these restrictions.

The Kaizen activity is often defined by: "We don't have that, we don't have this," and so forth. The point is that we overcome these limitations by doing Kaizen. **"If you can't generate the money, generate the ideas!"**

To implement ideas successfully, we must first recognize that there are real limitations, that there are restrictions—but we still plan to make improvements! In many companies where Kaizen is practiced, they don't clearly explain this third and critical definition of **Kaizen: to make an improvement within the restrictions.** This is usually because the company is still following traditional suggestions systems. In the past, when companies introduced a suggestion system they would say, "We want you to bring up many ideas, as much as possible...and the company will take care of im-

65

plementing your ideas." This sounds very nice, but often it's just not possible. Part of that reason may be because the ideas are often very costly and could require high technology.

Meanwhile, employees can get frustrated from hearing responses like "We are in the process of reviewing," while their ideas are accumulating and nothing appears to be happening with them. Truth is, often the people making the suggestions don't always pay attention to the costs or the need for higher technology, etc. In other words, they ignore the limitations. These suggestions leave the company asking, "How can we possibly implement those ideas?"

Exactly. To implement those ideas, we must find ways to either overcome these obstacles or find other ways to work within our limitations. **If the ideas are not practical in meeting the reality, then those ideas are only wishes.**

"We have been doing well in the past." This man is sitting on his experience and success in the past.

The Idea Generator – Quick and Easy Kaizen

"I am told to do this."

"We always did this."

Kaizen requires us to adapt to the situation. There are people who do not understand this. They come up with the various reasons why they cannot. For example:

- **Our company has too many branches**
- **We produce such a variety of products**
- **Our products are really diversifying**
- **The change is too rapid**
- **We are not in a mass production situation**
- **Our people are too busy**

We've met all of these people over time, and you've probably met many of them yourself. **They are very good at listing the reasons why they cannot make a change.** Yet, other people who work within the same conditions may use these same reasons to the opposite end:

- **Therefore, we need improvement**
- **Therefore, we have room for improvement**
- **Therefore, we can come up with many ideas**

People who are good at Kaizen know that the above reasons are exactly what help them to make improvements. And those people who are good at listing all the reasons they cannot are really advertising how much they lack in ability and a willingness to do new things.

"Busy, busy, difficult, difficult. There is never enough time to make all the changes." "Wake up! The world is changing!"

Summary

1. Practical restrictions can be the catalyst for Quick and Easy Kaizen: Time, people, leadership/management, money, equipment, and company culture.

2. Kaizen must overcome the restrictions. Adopt these new philosophies: "Since we don't have the money and we don't have the time, let's do Kaizen." "Let's think about ways to improve the method without spending money." "Let's think about the methods we can improve without spending too much time."

Chapter 5: Continuous Change

"But, we're just at the tip of the iceberg.
I think there are just tremendous opportunities.
There are a lot of companies that just choose not
to leverage the full resources available to them."
Joe Magliochetti, Chairman
and CEO, Dana Corporation

Sometimes people ask us, " Where is the division between our jobs and Kaizen?" Completing the objectives of our job descriptions is, of course, the essence, and is arguably the most important part of our jobs. After all, we receive our salary or wages in return. However, **it is also our responsibility to do our jobs in the best way possible. If we can find a way to do the same job more easily, more comfortably, and with greater quality and productivity, shouldn't we do just that?**

We need to select the best means by which to do our jobs, and we need to change our methods of doing our jobs, whenever it will help us to do our jobs better. That is Kaizen.

Kaizen is more than a pep talk

Kaizen is to change the way we do our jobs. It is changing the method of how we get things done every day. We improve safety measures by changing our methods, or we reduce costs by changing our methods. We can improve productivity by changing our methods, or improve customer service by changing our methods.

But very little will improve at all if we do not improve the method itself.

Kaizen cannot be done just through a pep talk. For example, in the past the words "customer service" and "customer satisfaction," became a fad in management circles. What happened afterward? What do we hear these days about customer service or customer satisfaction? In many companies, the customer service movement ended with just mere slogans. (Call some of the telephone companies and see how quickly you can find a "live" person to talk to you.)

However, there are some companies where the customer service movement really took root and resulted in lasting, positive change for the organization. The difference is that these companies had changed their methods, not simply their mottos

Merely encouraging people to do a better job in service relies on each worker's individual attitude and the spirit in which they serve customers, not to mention what his or her individual idea of "good service" might be. These things are bound to fluctuate. And while one employee may offer outstanding service to his customers, another might not at all, and once a customer receives unfair service from one employee, chances are he won't trust any of your employees.

One day I went to Nordstrom's men's clothing department to buy a shirt as a gift for a friend of mine. After making my selection, an attractive blue shirt, I brought it to the cash register desk. But when I got to the desk, the manager of that department was already serving another customer. He was talking with her and was also making a phone call regarding her needs. I thought I would just have to wait until he completed serving this other person.

But to my pleasant surprise, while he continued to talk on the telephone, he took the shirt from me and also my credit card, then rang up the transaction, placed the shirt into a box, put the box into a shopping bag, indicated for me to sign the credit slip, gave me a receipt, and waved goodbye. It was the first time that I saw someone able to so easily serve two customers so well at the same time. He had changed his method so simply to serve his customers better.

We've all heard the expression, "The end justifies the means." It's easy to say when we like our results! However, we should consider whether the result is because of mere luck or whether it was achieved by good methods and good means.

If you did not have good methods then your results were probably based on luck. Maybe you will not have the same luck next time, instead it could turn out to be a disaster. To avoid those disasters from happening, it is better to have an exact method that works, one that "justifies the end." If something does go wrong, you can study the process mindfully so that next time you can change the method.

Be careful!

> **"Take care of the means and the**
> **end will take care of itself."**
> **M. K. Ghandhi**

The same thing is true when dealing with accidents and problems in general. Where people don't practice Kaizen by changing methods, you will often hear people saying things like "be careful," and "pay more attention." Those words are repeated over and over because the conditions never change.

When accidents happen, people say, "we will never repeat this again," or "this shouldn't happen again." And it shouldn't. But if you change the method, and do Kaizen in those workplaces, at least you can avoid repeating the same problem. That means progress.

Kaizen means continuous change

As they say, if you are put into a corner, you can figure a way out. In most cases, this is true; if you find yourself in a difficult situation you can generally expect to do things better, somehow. But that is not always true. Sometimes it seems you just can't do anything to get out of that corner. When this is the case, chances are that the situation does not have a built in method for change.

If you could change something about your circumstance, then you may be able to get out of the difficult situation. Perhaps a better expression would be: **"If you are put in a corner, change something!"** If you are put into a difficult situation, try to change something—at least one small thing. If you can change just one thing, you may be able to get out of the corner you feel you are in.

In Kaizen, **changes need not be big to be effective.** We only need to change the method on a small scale. Therefore, we can do this quickly and easily. However, the key is to continue this effort. To do this, we cannot just install our Kaizens and stop there. It is important to write them down, observe the impact, and share our ideas with others.

Excuse you – never me!

It is funny that when other people make mistakes we are often very sensitive and we might respond quickly and get upset. However, when we make mistakes ourselves, we are usually not so sensitive about them. We have a wonderful capacity to excuse ourselves almost instantaneously.

But it's a far better thing to view all mistakes with a "no blame" attitude—it's more productive anyway. Try looking at the mistakes as only opportunities to improve. We should look at those mistakes from a slight distance, like a doctor or a scientist. We want to find a solution, not to fix the blame. That is how Kaizen works.

So when mistakes do happen, we step back and look carefully at the method being used to see what change can be made in the method. The following figures describe a good example. Type A part was being assembled. There are similar parts, type A and type B, in the same box. The workers could easily make a mistake by picking up the wrong part. In that case, telling someone to just "be careful" is not good enough.

Using Kaizen, the worker decided to add a placard to cover each half of the box, with a big "A" and "B" character on the opposite sides. So when the worker intends to pick up part A, part B is covered with a placard labeled "B." Since there is no chance for part B to get picked up from the box, there can be no mistake!

This was not a change in method handed down from upper management; this was a change thought up and implemented directly by the worker, the results of which benefited the entire company.

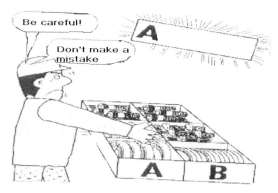

High chance to make a mistake before improvement.

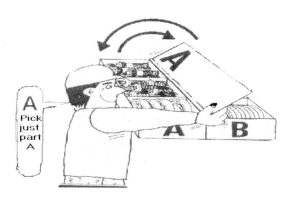

Workers can easily pick up just part A after improvement.

The Idea Generator – Quick and Easy Kaizen

Summary

1. If you are in a difficult situation, change something. One small change may be all it takes to find the way out of a "corner."

2. If you want lasting change, you must change your method, not just your motto.

Part II

Kaizen Steps and Principles Through Practical Examples. Including the Methods on Writing Quick and Easy Kaizen Memo

Part II Overview

The three most important questions we must answer in this section are:

- **How can you write down and share improvements quickly?**
- **How can you implement improvement quickly?**
- **How can you bring improvement ideas to the surface continuously?**

Why do we need to spend so much time just answering these three points?

Kaizen is implementation-oriented and needs to be brought to the surface through appropriate documentation.

Implementing Kaizen improvements is extremely important to motivate employees to excel in their work and for a company to maintain its competitiveness.

```
+-----------------------------------------+
|                 Kaizen                  |
|                                         |
|             Implementation              |
|                                         |
|    Surfacing through documentation      |
+-----------------------------------------+
```

Employees automatically come up with ideas when they want to see things changed or improved. But in most cases, these ideas become little more than a wish list. Even in companies where a suggestion system is in place, when a suggestion is made from an employee's wish list, most often nothing happens. And if nothing happens when suggestions are made, employees soon lose interest in the system and neglect to submit ideas again.

This neglect leads to frustration, and the feeling that nothing they say is important or will make a difference. "If no one's going to listen to me, I will just do my job and collect my pay? Why bother making suggestions when they're always ignored?"

The powerful difference is that Quick and Easy Kaizen does much more than pass ideas and suggestions on to management—it is **a complete idea implementation system**. It teaches people how to continuously bring their ideas to the surface, to effectively move their improvement ideas beyond paper, to get the ideas approved by their supervisors, and to install the ideas by themselves or with their work team. And now we will show you how you can begin using Kaizen quickly and easily.

Chapter 6: Kaizen Improvement Activities

*". . . it is always the simple
that produces the
marvelous."*
Amelia Barr

What stops us from improving continuously? Why do we get stuck in old or comfortable ways of doing things? What is it we're afraid of? Is it really human nature to resist change? The goal of this chapter is to show you how to start simply and bring small changes into your work environment–to help you get started changing and making improvements. Soon it will become second nature to you.

Many companies have suffered in promoting improvement activities. They find it difficult to come up with ideas on how to continuously foster improvement involving every employee. In the following pages you will find some simple but powerful tools that will help you to utilize Quick and Easy Kaizen. But first, let us recognize these **3 rules to implementing Kaizen:**

1. **Stop.** Stop doing things that you have done in the past but don't seem to have any real reason to do today.

2. **Reduce.** Eliminate unnecessary things that may be cluttering the workplace and cut back on activities that are not fully required today.

3. **Change.** Just do something different. Make one slight improvement to make something better.

Oftentimes employees are introduced to what might be called trouble-shooting types of improvements. **Most often, people feel that these improvement activities are something they must do in addition to their normal work,** and they grow to resent the activities. They believe that as long as they are doing what is asked of them and there are no problems, there is no need to make improvements.

However, we all know that change is occurring today more rapidly than ever before. **Continuous improvement is a part of industry, so it must also be a part of our jobs.** To stay competitive, we must all constantly improve.

I keep a 'to-do' list and work on it daily. During the day whenever I get an idea I write it down on the back of my to-do list or on any scratch of paper available. Each morning before I start working on my various projects, I take yesterday's to-do list and the scraps of paper with my notes and update a new to-do list. I put a three-digit number in front of each item on the list to prioritize the list, and then I sort it. I then try to accomplish the items on the list starting at the top, the highest priority. Gradually the list would grow longer and longer, and I would have items on the list that had been there for maybe over a year, sitting there on the list unaccomplished. I wanted to do them all but I just couldn't find the time, or I would be stymied because the project is too challenging or new for me. As an example, I wanted to create a web page, but this required me to read several books and to learn how to do it first. Since I have never created a web page, in my mind it was large project and could wait out its priority, so I kept putting it off.

But, now I am determined to follow the instructions in this book and do Quick and Easy Kaizen to slowly, little by little, over-come the mental hurdles and attack each item on my to-do list. So, I finally started to produce a web page, and hopefully it will be accessible to you as you read this book. I have also reduced the to-do list enormously—doing one Kaizen after the next.

Learning only from past experience – the wrong way

There are plenty of opportunities for all of us to make im-provements in our own workplace, many opportunities to improve our own jobs. But if those improvements are outside of our own job responsibilities, we must rely on managers and supervisors to support them and hope that other people are willing to install those ideas.

The goal of the Quick and Easy Kaizen System is to show management and employees how it is possible to come up with new ideas, make improvements, and install them one after the other either by themselves or in conjunction with other members of their work teams. We do not consider improvements as a tempo-rary activity done by only a few people in the company.

Even if you don't currently have a formal system in place, ac-tual improvements are happening all the time in the work place. People are just doing them naturally as they perform their work. **The problem is that usually a company is unable to sustain or expand these improvement activities throughout the company.**

For example, when there is a problem or an accident happens in the workplace, a company thinks of a way to work together to make a change, and then they ask the employees to improve based on that change. At such a time some improvement will occur; people are wary. However, once that particular problem appears to be solved, and people are thanked for their efforts, everyone stops thinking about improvement activities, and that's usually the end of it—until the next problem comes along.

I remember my first visit to a cable manufacturer in Connecticut. I was invited by the plant manager to see if I could suggest ways for them to improve the quality of their products. As I walked around the plant, I noticed a young lady working at a machine that allowed her to spin two cables at the same time. She was fast and highly skilled.

I was introduced to the operator and began talking to her questioning her about the quality of the cables being produced. I asked her if she had ever found any defects? She immediately replied that when she first came to the plant around nine years earlier, she noticed some defects on a cable and immediately stopped the machine. She then wrote up a red tag and placed it on the cable and went back to work spinning more cable. She related that a short while later her supervisor came by, noticed the red tag, yanked it off the cable and said, "What are you trying to do, take away the job of the quality manager? Your job is to spin the cable and his job is to find the defects."

So this young operator learned a hard lesson. It is true that most often employees without Kaizen training suggest things that are beyond their authority. In other words, they suggest things for their boss or for others to accomplish, instead of themselves. Of *course, there is a place for those kinds of activities—to get impor-tant things accomplished. However, what we want to emphasize here in this book is that we can **improve those things within our own authority and area of responsibility, and that everyone has the ability to make changes happen**.*

This situation the operator found herself in existed in many companies as quality once was left in the hands of the quality manager only. But today quality improvement is everyone's job. Under Kaizen, we want everyone to be responsible for quality im-provement.

It was different in the past!

Not so long ago, in the heart of any American town, you were sure to find a local butcher shop, a small bakery, a small fruit store and other small stores to shop at. Today, it seems only the large supermarkets survive.

As well, whenever a person was sick the doctor would drive to the house, any day, any time of the day or night to attend to the patient's needs. And now, you are lucky to find a doctor who is taking new patients, lucky if you can make an appointment at their office, and luckier still if they can spend more than 10 minutes with you. What's more, have you heard of any doctor's recently calling their patients at home to see if they've healed?

My doctor

Nowadays, everything, almost every profession is rapidly changing. Travel agents, insurance brokers, bookkeepers, stock-brokers, are all conducting their businesses differently from just a few years back. It seems that no profession is sacred. (If it is, then wait a few moments and it's sure to change.)

Instead of change coming to you unconsciously, we suggest a new system for you to consciously adapt to change as it happens. You become the master of your destiny.

In Japan, everyone has a hanko, a portable stamp, to put their mark on official documents. This is done at banks, for example, and almost every legal document requires this stamp. On our last trip to Japan, my wife, who is Japanese, wanted to open a bank account, but she left her hanko at home and the bank would not open the account.

Even in America, at one time companies felt that in order for every business document to look and feel official, it must have a rubber stamp with the date and the name of the person who initiated the document. Finally someone realized that the stamp was no longer necessary.

The Idea Generator – Quick and Easy Kaizen

All we need now is our signature, which we all "carry" with us, at all times. What's more, you can lose your stamp, while you will always have your signature.

Why is it so hard to sustain and expand improvement activities?

Many companies have suffered in their attempts to promote improvement activities. They find it difficult to come up with ideas on how to continuously foster improvement and involve every employee. Also, the design of many improvement activities can leave some employees feeling burdened with additional work or unappreciated when their ideas are not implemented. **More importantly, if the activities are temporary and sporadic, then the activities won't mean much to the whole organization.**

To the average employee, **Quick and Easy Kaizen seems only a small thing to add to the routine. And when all employees are involved in improvement activities, on a regular and continuous basis, it becomes powerful and meaningful for the entire company.**

But in order for these many small changes to have that major impact, everyone must be involved, and everyone must contribute. Like baseball or any team sport, we should expect everyone to do his or her best, and to get even better. All it takes is one person to choose not to participate, or "drop the ball," and then the whole team loses.

The old suggestion system

The initial suggestion system in the United States was credited to the Kodak Corporation. The first recorded suggestion in 1898 at Kodak came from a worker who wrote, "Clean the windows." You see, in those days factories were naturally lit, and so clean windows brightened the workplace. It was a simple idea that was not at all difficult to do.

"Clean the windows"
First suggestion at Kodak in 1898

The purpose of the suggestion system was to help empower the worker, to begin to tap into their ideas, to ask them to use their brains in addition to their brawn, to help make the organization more participative, to get the workers more involved in solving day-to-day problems, and to let them share in the responsibility for the success of the company.

The first idea of, "Clean the windows," may seem incredibly simple to us now. But this new suggestion system was a major step in America. Up to that time workers generally were only told what to do; they were certainly never asked for their ideas. Ideas were solely to come down from management—for it was management's responsibility to think about improvement, not the workers.

It probably didn't help at the time that a good percentage of the labor force was made up of immigrants who were mostly unable to speak the language. These factory workers used their hands and were not expected to use their brains, and of course, no one really cared about their hearts. Their suggestions, if any, were only seen as additional work for their supervisors.

That's why managers did not encourage employee suggestions and instead became accustomed to looking only at the big ideas. To make it worthwhile pursuing, supervisors and suggestion system managers were only interested in those ideas that would represent substantial savings to the company. As a result, employees learned quickly not to put in what management would consider small, insubstantial ideas.

This suggestion system was often burdensome to the supervisor who felt it was his responsibility to come up with the method to install the improvement, not the worker. Often when a worker did come up with an improvement idea, the supervisor would "shoot it down," and find some reason to dampen the worker's enthusiasm. "It is too small an idea! It's a dumb idea, go back to work and do your job!"

We have found that there are people who can always find fault with an idea. They have an amazing talent that way.

Remember the old suggestion box? We had one a long time ago in our company until one day I looked inside and read, "Get rid of the suggestion box, nobody ever really looks at them."

Somehow the Kodak system shifted from a participative suggestion system to solely a cost-saving system. In many American companies, workers receive 10% to 20% of the cost savings from their suggestions. This requires a lot of accounting and evaluating, and feedback is often delayed.

When the Kodak system went from an employee-participation system to a cost-savings system, Kodak had to set up a suggestion office and a process to determine the exact saving's benefit to the company and the reward to be given to the worker. And suggestions dropped off dramatically.

In contrast, Dana offers very little as a reward for the ideas submitted by workers. The idea system is simply part of the worker's job and provides a real sense of achievement and recognition. Normally ideas submitted are responded to within 24 hours. When a worker's idea is accepted and applied, the employee feels a sense of involvement and discovers a new level of communication. There is also more respect between management and the workforce. Moreover, where the average suggestion system in America gets only one idea per worker in writing every seven years, Dana receives an average of over 24 ideas per worker per year. Something is clearly working. And that something is Kaizen.

I remember when I ran a data processing company and people would stand in line outside my office door waiting to present a problem for me to solve. I thought it was my job to solve all those

The Idea Generator – Quick and Easy Kaizen

problems, and I thought I had to find the time to do it or else the company would just stop. But if I'd understood the situation better at the time, I could have allowed others to grow by simply asking them to come up with the solution to the problem, by listening to them carefully, encouraging them to do the right thing and tell me what they did or what they intended to do.

Quick and Easy Kaizen memo system

With Quick and Easy Kaizen, the person who comes up with the idea installs it, and writes it up to share with others.

Exhibit 6-1 Small Kaizen made by frontline worker

Before improvement:	After improvement:
It took two people to lift the large and soft cover off the wash pit.	Added a chain with two ends fixed on the appropriate portion on the cover
Effect: It takes only one person now to lift the cover. **Submitted By**: E. T.	

Exhibit 6-1 is a very simple case, but just imagine the feeling the worker gets when the idea is accepted, installed, and recognized. Also imagine when you get an average of more than 24 of these ideas from every employee in the company, each year. It looks like:

They liked our ideas!

The old-style suggestion system began to change in Japan in the early 1970s, when it was recognized that allowing people to submit a lot of ideas would improve the quality of the products and foster greater involvement by people in their jobs. Consequently, American industry got hit hard in the late 1970s and early 1980s, and we finally realized that something was happening in Japan to make them so much more competitive. They were not only making small, fuel-efficient automobiles to compete with us; they were making products with much higher quality, at lower costs and with greater appeal to America's consumers.

In1981, I started to lead American managers on industrial study missions to Japan. On a plant visit to Japan, in February 1981, I visited the Toyota Motor Company. They were receiving around 70 improvement ideas in writing per worker per year, while in America it was still around only one idea every seven years. The Japanese system was so unusual that the members on my mission, 19 top U.S. managers, couldn't get a handle on what was really happening.

Toyota allowed the worker to submit any improvement idea no matter what the cost savings was to the company. And feedback from their supervisor was almost immediate. What's more, each manufacturing plant provided both employee training and a desig-nated person to manage the idea process.

As we walked around the Toyota plant, we were shown many of the small examples installed by the workers. But we still could not imagine how to administer a program like this in America.

The Idea Generator – Quick and Easy Kaizen

We were confused. What do you do when a worker submits ideas for improvements that can only be done by others, and those others are busy on their own?

And then there was the problem of what happens when the employee submits an idea that is rejected? Won't he feel rejected? And won't his creative flow stop with the thought, "Why bother? No one wants to hear what I have to say, so I will just do my job."

As we eventually learned, there are ways to keep ideas flowing even if a worker's idea is rejected, which we will explore further in this book.

Let's review a typical idea system, similar to the one at Dana. An employee gets an idea, writes it down, and posts the idea on the bulletin board for others to see. We want others to see the idea because other workers might be faced with a similar situation and the idea could help them also make improvements.

For example, at Dana, either the plant manager or a facilitator collects ideas daily, reviews the ideas, and returns them to the originator within 24 hours. A vast improvement over the old traditional system where it could take weeks, if not months, for feedback.

In a traditional suggestion system, a worker may implement some of the ideas herself, but some are installed by other workers in the same department or another department, or by engineers—or even by management. **If managed properly**[*], this kind of system can be very effective because some of the ideas submitted, even

---

[*] See Dana interviews in Part IV

93

those submitted for others to do, could be quite valuable to the company. This system has a place. But we are really addressing something else in this book—similar but slightly different.

We are primarily concerned in helping the worker establish a Kaizen mindset to always, if possible, focus on continuous improvement.

Exhibit 6-2 Kaizen to improve eye bolts

Before improvement: Chain would sometimes come off the eyebolts.	After improvement: I put a safety hook on the latch.
Effect: Hook can't come out. **Submitted By**:	

There are companies that do have a Kaizen system, or something similar, that encourages workers to come up with many improvement ideas and write them down, or to document the Kaizen after implementing it, not just do it and forget about it, but to document it and share them with their fellow workers. This is an evolution from the traditional suggestion system. This Kaizen system has real "power" and should not be thought of as just a variation of an old theme. Companies like Dana have recognized that real creative power is locked within every single worker, and if management taps into that creativity both the worker and the company benefits. Ask Joe Magliochetti, chairman of Dana, what his most competitive corporate power is. We're sure he will respond that his "idea" or Kaizen system leads the way.

Improvement Report

Why do you document it?

The Idea Generator – Quick and Easy Kaizen

If you actually go through the visualization process to study and create new improvement ideas, to write them down and document the improvement, and then share them with others, you will notice a wonderful effect takes place.

First, if you look around carefully, you will notice that many of the workplace improvements that have been made are often visible just at a glance. You can see what has changed and where, and who is installing what kind of improvement with ease.

Second, if you stop and ask people to tell you about some of the ideas that they had installed, you will immediately notice the personal pride the employees feel about being allowed to fully participate in the improvement process. Since the average employee in a Quick and Easy Kaizen environment has installed a lot of ideas, they will have much to tell you. This is very powerful. Instead of people feeling that they are just "cogs" in the wheel, they now feel like important members in the company.

An important aspect to keep in mind is whether the improvement is just a one-time event with people treating it like that, or do they make improvements and then keep coming up with better ideas? Rather than just making one improvement and going on with their work, people using a written Kaizen or Improvement report system (i.e. Kaizen memo) help to make it more visible by sharing their ideas with their fellow workers and allowing others to look at the documented improvement reports. When using a documentation system, you have the foundation for continuous improvements involving everyone.

Often people complain when we try to implement this Quick and Easy Kaizen system. "We are already busy. Why do we have to do this cumbersome thing, write it down? Why do we have to write it down? We have already done it! Why do you need us to report this?"

Companies who have successfully changed to a Kaizen system **explain why everyone must write it down when they introduce the system.** Oftentimes, however, despite their initial effort to explain it, they still cannot sustain it. Somehow it becomes a numbers game. You are given the target, the quota, and employees feel like they are forced to improve to meet the targeted numbers. This is not Kaizen; it is a situation to be avoided!

The terminology of new system

A suggestion is an idea about something we would like to change in the future. The term 'implemented suggestion,' is confusing because as soon as something is implemented it is no longer a suggestion.

It is understandable that many people use certain words and expressions, such as implemented suggestion, simply out of habit. But we would like the people who are promoting improvement to consider changing their language. It might just be a habit, but using the word 'suggestions' does not always convey the precise meaning to others. It is possible that others are not as familiar with the concept. When this aspect is pointed out, people tend to say, "Well, in our system, we still allow 'un-implemented suggestions,' or 'not-yet implemented suggestions.' Therefore, we cannot remove the word 'suggestions' from our corporate vocabulary." This is a problem because it might be misleading. Of course, everything has exceptions. But in this explanation they are using the name of the exception as their mainstream system. We believe that the proper way should be to use the mainstream as a name and treat exceptions as exceptions.

We recommend that you **use the name Quick and Easy Kaizen, or Implemented Idea System,** or something that captures the notion of workers submitting ideas to be implemented by themselves—and not suggestions for others to do.

Just imagine how much more powerful you would feel about implementing your own improvement idea as opposed to making a suggestion and seeing someone else install it and gather all of the recognition. Wouldn't you rather install the idea yourself and share it with others, and give them the opportunity to do the same thing? **There is a great sense of achievement in the doing.**

The Documentation Process

First, let's discuss why or what do we need to document. And, more importantly, why we want to promote improvement activities at all.

There are 3 reasons why we should have a Quick and Easy Kaizen system for improvement activities, why you should also make improvements visible, and document those improvements.

1. To make the system as a conscious effort.

Going back to the earlier example of my own office, I've found that if I can just stop for a few moments and look around, there are many things that can be improved that don't get done. There are always other things that are considered more important to do than to just straighten up. Even though mistakes are repeatedly made, I always figure that it is still more important to focus on the important things than to stop and fix permanently the little annoying mistakes. However, the reality is that these little mistakes continually pop up and if I would seriously count the hours those mistakes waste in a year, I would be overwhelmed.

For example, I waste an enormous amount of paper with my printer. This printer has four different paper trays. I often have to change the tray selection instruction when I print. When I make a mistake and select the wrong tray, I just throw away the wasted paper and then go in and modify the tray selection and do it again. It is a little frustrating but I figure it is easier to just print again than to stop and figure out a new way of not making the same mistake over and over again.

Finally, with Quick & Easy Kaizen, I discovered that my HP printer and Microsoft Word software had a conflict. The printer menu does not control the print operation. But, if I go to Page Setup in Word, I can select the proper tray to use and it takes precedence over the Print menu. I just have to remember to go to the Print Setup first. This new method will save me a lot of time and eliminate a lot of waste.

Self-inspection

This is very similar to the quality inspection technique developed by Dr. Shigeo Shingo, the creator of the Toyota Just-In-Time (JIT) system. He called one of his techniques "Self Inspection," whereby he encouraged workers to just double check their work every time they did something.

The Idea Generator – Quick and Easy Kaizen

We all need reminders to make conscious efforts. Once we do something we tend to just do it over and over again without thinking. It can work for us often but sometimes it can lead to unexpected problems.

Recently, at a supermarket overseas, I was watching a cashier ring up my groceries. He would enter the item number and then go back and mentally reenter it again. He did that on every single item. He rechecked his entry every single time. It slowed things down a bit, but it insured that my bill would be correct. It was simple, maybe too simple, but I thought it was just great. I very rarely see this at supermarkets where the cashier relies on the bar code scanner or they enter the item number or an amount but they do neglect to double check.

2. To ensure that improvement activities continue.

We all need some form of reminders to do things consciously. Nordstrom department stores have an excellent reputation for quality customer service. Great customer service does not happen accidentally. The manager of every Nordstrom store gets on the microphone every single day 10-minutes before the store opens to talk to all the employees and remind them to work on improving customer service. They might read a customer compliment or a customer complaint. **They know that if they do not remind employees every single day to focus on pleasing customers that people tend to forget.**

Dana Corporation has one person at each plant or office whose job it is to promote the idea system. In some smaller plants, the job of promoter is also the plant manager's job. In other, larger plants there is at least one individual whose prime responsibility is to promote the idea process. The plant manager or the promoter responsible for the idea system goes around the plant at the end of every single day to gather the ideas submitted by the workers. The manager or the promoter will read every single idea submitted and make sure that the worker gets a response to their ideas within 24 hours.

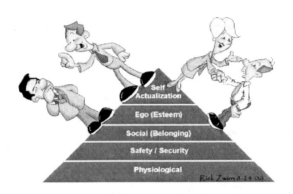

Maslow's hierarchy of human needs

Here is a diagram of psychologist Abraham Maslow's Motivational Theory or Hierarchy of Needs. Maslow felt that, to motivate people, you must appeal to people on their level of needs, from the most basic and physical to the highest intellectual levels of needs. For example, to motivate a hungry person you provide him an opportunity to earn enough money to feed himself. But, once that level is satisfied, once he is fed, you can no longer motivate him by appealing to him on the same level that was just satisfied; you must appeal to a higher need. Once hunger is satisfied, you can motivate a person by appealing to his need for safety and security, and so on up the levels of the hierarchy. According to Maslow's theory, once all of the lower needs—physiological, safety/security, social (belonging), and ego (esteem)—are fulfilled, people can still be continuously motivated if they are given opportunities to be self-actualized.

We can define self-actualization as "the achievement of one's full potential through creativity, independence, spontaneity, and a grasp of the real world." People can be highly motivated if they have the opportunity to express themselves through their own ideas. **Self-actualization is conscious growth.** Conscious growth comes from your ideas to solve your current problem. Kaizen allows that to happen.

For many years I taught a data processing management course for the American Management Associations. I read and studied Abraham Maslow's Motivational Theory or Hierarchy of Needs. I liked it and so did my audience of managers because we all wanted to know how to motivate others. Even though I taught this hierarchy to many people, I didn't really understand for years what the top rung of the ladder, labeled "Self-Actualization," really meant. After learning about Quick and Easy Kaizen, I think that I do understand it now.

3. To see the improvement process becomes an organization-wide effort involving every worker.

Of course, there are always individual employees who will come up with improvement ideas without a formal system. But if we want to compete at an international level today, we must develop a process to foster improvement from everyone. Just look at the excitement generated from the Internet. Look into the Internet companies and you will see almost the entire workforce sitting in front of their computer screens creating new software. Yes, money is one of their strong motivators, but just being part of a swiftly growing company and being allowed to express themselves creatively drives these workers to spend long hours way into the night and on almost every weekend, driving themselves and being grateful to be part of that very exciting change process.

Well, in America and throughout the world, there are still vast numbers of the old types of jobs with people working in factories, offices, and stores, doing very repetitive, uncreative jobs. What are their chances to be self-actualized? Are these jobs really any less important than those in the new exciting industries? Or have circumstances in their life just placed them into so-called "limited" jobs?

If we look at companies like Dana and others that have installed an idea system, particularly a Kaizen system, we can see a whole new level of excitement take place at the work site. **What a great feeling it is to come up with an idea that improves your work! What a great feeling it is when the boss comes over and tells you how wonderful that idea of yours was! What a wonderful feeling it is when you see other people picking up your idea and using it to improve their own jobs!**

We want to ensure that Kaizen becomes an organization-wide improvement process. We want everyone to be involved. We want one new idea to feed another idea. We want one Kaizen to trigger another Kaizen. We want continuous improvement. Often Kaizen is made analogous to the spiraling colorful pole seen in front of a Barber Shop, symbolizing one idea continuously building on top of the previous idea. The spinning is endless and the number of improvement ideas is also endless.

Kaizen Means to do Ordinary Things in an Ordinary Way

*"I have learned the novice can often
see things that the expert overlooks.
All that is necessary is not to be
afraid of making mistakes, or of
appearing naive."*
Abraham Maslow

Some jobs can be effective by doing them in a centralized manner; while for others, decentralization may be better. The situation determines whether a centralized or decentralized way will get the best result. And getting the best results is Kaizen.

One company had to ship items into different places. Originally, when they had few branches and factories, only one person was needed to do the entire shipping job. However, as the number of branches and factories increased it was beyond one person's ability. There were increased problems with sending items to the wrong place, so they changed to a decentralized system instead. It was necessary to have multiple people doing this job, and each had his own designated place to ship items to. They now pick up the things only for their specific location, which has eliminated the problem of sending things to the wrong place. By changing the method as a means to change the situation, this transformation could be classified as a Kaizen.

In another company, the employees were borrowing videos and digital cameras and so forth. When the there were only a few of these items to begin with, it was sufficient to just use a written note to record when someone was checking out the equipment or returning it. However, when the numbers increased, the written note alone was not enough to manage this checking in and out. So they began to use a big board to record the information instead. The new system allowed people to see the status of what was in or out at a glance. Furthermore, everybody knew which item was where, who had it and for how much longer he or she would have it. This is also Kaizen; these people changed the method to improve the situation. .

Exhibit 6-3 A new method to control video camera inventory

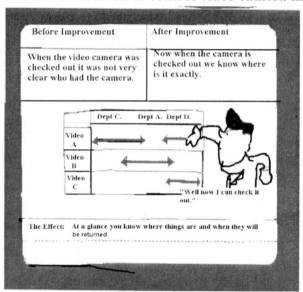

It's common sense; it's obvious; it's ordinary

When we say these are good examples of Kaizen, some people argue: "How in the world can you call that Kaizen? That is so obvious, so ordinary." Sometimes when a Kaizen example is simple, they tend to insist it is natural, obvious, common sense and so forth: "Why do you call these things Kaizen? Why don't they just do these things as part of their normal job?" If you're having any of these thoughts, we would like to assure you—you're right on track! As we've been saying all along, Kaizen IS simple; it IS obvious; and with any luck, it WILL become an ordinary part of your employees' jobs!   But if we stop to ask "why now?" or "why didn't you do this sooner?", no one would ever try to do Kaizen twice.   Many people, especially at a managerial level, have the misconception that Kaizen means to do something beyond the ordinary. Somehow they believe that which is considered obvious, ordinary, and common sense is of little value or importance. So these, people who insist that Kaizen is to do something beyond this level of ordinary tend to criticize the small ideas as being just ordinary things, not Kaizen.

"Why is this a Kaizen? It is so simple and obvious! Why did you do it now? You should have done this much earlier."

A very confused manager

On the other hand, a company that promotes Kaizen very well does not criticize small ideas that are ordinary things. They are more concerned whether those ordinary, common sense things are really being implemented and practiced. They are not concerned about the standard they establish in their head of what is common sense or ordinary. They are really concerned about what is reality and whether the ideas are practiced correctly.

Look squarely at reality

At many workplaces, everybody knows what **should** be done. However, there might still be a better way to do it. Moreover, those things that everybody knows should be done are often not practiced correctly in reality. **The reality is that ordinary things are not always done well,** especially in a busy workplace.

So, if you notice this unfavorable situation, and you notice the need to implement those ordinary things, by doing that you can reduce the number of problems. And that is Kaizen. Instead of asking "Why now?" you will hear people say "Thank you for noticing that; thank you for doing that." In a good Kaizen environment you hear those words more often.

If the central control system doesn't work, why not use a decentralized control method? If notes at the control system are not working, why not use a display board? Of course, you could say these things are common sense. But in reality, it's when these things are not practiced and that you have a problem. If you can do these ordinary practices, regularly, that is Kaizen.

The Best is the Enemy of Kaizen

*"A mistake is simply another way
of doing things."*
Katharine Graham

Strive for the best, but start by getting better.

There is a common problem encountered in many workplaces, and even in some homes: forgetting to turn off the lights! One place we visited had a simple addition of pinwheels and ribbons to visually remind people to shut off the lights as they left. When we talk about improving this situation by adding ribbons or pinwheels, inevitably someone argues, "Well, that is not perfect. It is not a complete solution. Maybe it will be effective for a while, but once they become accustomed to the new method, people will still forget to turn off the lights off. So it's no good."

To those who think that way, we would like to offer this maxim: "The best is the enemy of Kaizen." Of course, we want to find the best solution, but the best solution usually doesn't come to us right away. And if we are always looking for the best solution, we end up doing nothing and the problem continues. That is to say, **if we are trying to do the best from the beginning, most often we cannot even get started**.

So, we must take small improvement steps, one by one. We must look for something *better*. We, too, recognize that the ribbons or pinwheels are not perfect solutions, but they are better than what the company had before. And they are a step in the right direction.

If you watched platform divers at the Olympics, you might have noticed water splashing the surface of the pool to break up the surface tension. That surface tension can actually hurt the divers as they break through the water into the pool. The little splash from a small hose breaks up the water's tension and makes it safer to dive in.

Like that water surface tension in an Olympic swimming pool, the resistance we feel from undertaking something is real, even though it may be invisible to us. Our resistance prevents us from changing, and the greater the undertaking the greater the resistance.

Of course, in our work we should be striving for perfection, striving for the best. But striving for the best and being entangled with what is the best are two separate things.

Those who are entangled or captured by the thought of being the best will accomplish very little in the greater scheme of things. You are entangled, restricted, not free to make gradual changes toward a better end. The method to be used for Kaizen is to start with trying to find "better ways," small simple changes you can do today, while you continue to strive for the best method.

Exhibit 6-4 Small Kaizen to serve customers better

Before improvement:	After improvement:
No exit emergency lights	Replaced the bulbs
Effect: The hallway is safer	
Submitted By: Elisa	

If there is such a thing as an absolute preventive method, say for forgetting to turn off switches, then that is the best. You might need a motion sensor, or maybe complete automation, and so forth, and that would solve the problem. However, normally these kinds of improvements cannot be done immediately because of the costs and the restrictions of technology. Those restrictions have to be cleared to make it happen. If there is a ribbon or pinwheel handy, you can attach it immediately. And since you can do it immediately, you get immediate results.

Of course, these cannot be said to be perfect solutions. **But in Kaizen, you don't have to be perfect. Rather than being perfect, you can start with the things you can do right now.** Kaizen is striving to get immediate results by making even a small difference by taking a small step.

> **In Kaizen you don't have to be perfect**
> **Kaizen strives to get immediate results**
> **By making a small difference**
> **By taking a small step**

We want to make improvement activities a habit, but to do so requires a small "push" to get started, and then follow-up to sustain it.

How many of you have 'wish lists' or long 'to-do' lists with many items that you never get around to taking care of? Perhaps

109

part of the problem is that you're still looking for "the best way" or "most complete way" of accomplishing these tasks. If the same items have been on your list for some time, perhaps you should start by doing these tasks "a *better* way" instead. For example, if you have "clean out the filing cabinet" on your list, but you can never find the time, start by cleaning out just one drawer of the cabinet. Instead of telling yourself you must clean out the entire cabinet all at once, set a more realistic goal for yourself such as cleaning out one drawer each week, or each month—whatever you *can* manage.

Start with the things you can do. Let's say we have ten problems in our work area. Maybe these are ten mistakes, or potential accidents, or *something*. To eliminate all ten in one stroke is probably very difficult, if not impossible. Maybe it would require you to change a whole machine, improve the equipment, do remodeling and so forth. It requires big changes and takes time and money. However, if you can make one little change on the machine, or the method can be changed quickly, you can expect to remove one problem out of ten, and that is Kaizen. Of course, we are not saying you should be content living with the other nine problems. We still have the nine problems and we still need other improvements.

Big changes, innovation, do not easily work out.

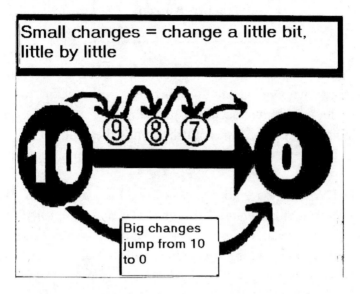

Kaizen. Start with what you can do now.
Small changes go from 10 to 9, 9 to 8, and 8 to 7 down to zero.

In the case of the ribbon, if the initial ribbon is not working very well, maybe you should change the color so it is easy to see. Or maybe you can change where you place the ribbon, or maybe the shape of it. By changing small things, you can expect to reduce the problems even further, from ten to nine and so forth. If you can eventually reduce the problem to zero that is wonderful. However, in the real world, things do not work that completely. There are many restrictions in our work environment. You will often "hit a wall" where you can no longer improve in this manner. If you hit the wall, then that's it. You can stop right there. You don't have to do what you cannot do. You should do what you can do.

> **Do what you can do.**
> **That is Kaizen.**

Those people who are not good at Kaizen try very hard to overcome what they cannot do. Since they are attacking what they cannot do, they cannot accomplish anything. Those, however, who are good at Kaizen, begin with the things they can do right away and do it. They do it to the extent they can, and they get results.

In Kaizen, we are not really looking for a big effect. **We are concerned about the small things that can make a little difference.** That's what we are doing in Kaizen. When you want to make big changes, it requires money and, of course, to that extent you can expect a bigger result. Therefore, the big changes come with big responsibility.

Looking for small things.

Exhibit 6-5 Small Kaizen made by airline stewardess

Before improvement:	After improvement:
Customer fell asleep	Placed a blanket over customer
Effect: The customer should have a more restful sleep. **Submitted By**: Mary	

The Idea Generator – Quick and Easy Kaizen

Of course, exhibit 6-5 is very small, but the Kaizen system does encourage people to make these very small improvements. Mary undoubtedly felt very proud of her idea and the result was very beneficial to the customer.

A Kaizen is a small change that you can make right now. If it improves the situation a little bit, then in most cases that would be satisfactory. As we said earlier, if you are striving for perfection, you cannot move, you are entangled. So, in that situation, remember the words "The best is the enemy of Kaizen." You might use this phrase to get away from the perfectionists.

In essence, we want people to be involved, excited, and challenged by their work. When they wake up Monday morning to go to work, we want them to feel that there are stimulating things for them to do in life. No matter what kind of work a person does, it can always be improved; that's the wonderful thing about Quick and Easy Kaizen: you, the worker, can "make a difference!" You do not have to always wait for someone else. You do it! You begin to find ways to make improvements! Believe us, there is great joy in discovering your inner talents to find new ways to make improvements in your very own job. So stop complaining that, "they won't let me!" And do it!

Summary

1.   **The goal in Quick and Easy Kaizen is to get everyone involved, not just a few people making improvements. We want the improvement process to last and not just be a temporary "Flavor of the month."**

2. We want to improve those things, within our own authority, and area of responsibility that you have to make changes happen.

3. Three reasons why we should have a Quick and Easy Kaizen documentation system for improvement activities:

- To make the system as a conscious effort. (Vital factor: self-motivation)
- To ensure that improvement activities continue. (Vital factor: small change to reduce the potential resistance)
- To see that the improvement process becomes an organization-wide effort involving every worker. (Vital factor: total participation)

4. We want the improvement system to be done:

- Consciously
- Continuously
- And involve all employees

5. We want employees to establish a Kaizen mindset to focus on continuous improvement.

6. Kaizen is:

- Ordinary
- Common
- Obvious

7. Start with "better," while striving for the best. By changing this way, you can do it right now when the best is something you cannot do right now; it is too much. Start with what you can do and go as far as you can.

Chapter 7: Surfacing Ideas

*"Make visible what, without
you, might perhaps never
have been seen."*
Robert Bresson

Surfacing is the Key to Making Quick and Easy Kaizen Visible

Surfacing Kaizen means simply writing the implemented idea on a Kaizen form and displaying it either on a bulletin board or putting it into notebooks where other employees can see the ideas. **Surfacing Kaizen is a process of sharing results throughout the company to inspire others** to also come up with and implement improvement ideas.

After reviewing our explanations and seeing many of the Kaizen examples, most people think, "I am relieved. Kaizen is just at that level. It is obvious; ordinary things are okay. We can imitate others. That is all right too. The more trivial the Kaizen is the better Kaizen is" and so on. In that manner they are beginning to understand how simple Kaizen is.

People also feel relieved when we show them Kaizen examples and they say, "We have many examples like that in our workplace." But often, once asked to write down their own Kaizens, their attitudes change suddenly. "It is cumbersome to write it down." "I am not good at writing things down." Those are the usual responses. They tend to say, "Since we have already implemented Kaizen, I think that is it. Why do we need to take the time to write it down?"

> **Kaizen has been done**
> **I don't like to write it down**
> **It is cumbersome to write it down**
> **Why do you need to write a Kaizen**
> **down anyway?**

You lose a valuable opportunity to share Kaizen with others when you don't encourage people to write it down on paper. If that happens, some people do Kaizen, and other people don't do Kaizen. In some situations, maybe your Kaizen activities become very popular temporarily and then die down quickly so that Kaizen doesn't last. You will end up with that kind of situation. Many companies, many organizations have experienced something like that. Here's how yours can do better: You write it down to sustain the activity. **It is constant doing and sharing that stimulates others to do it.**

However, there is a lot of resistance in organizations to writing it down. Implementation of Kaizen has been done to some extent in most companies, but often they just stopped there, and therefore the activity over time does not last long or does not expand throughout the organization.

Kaizen, as we talked about earlier, is small changes. If only a partial amount of your workforce is doing that or if you do it only temporarily, Kaizen activity will never be a part of the power of your company. To continue Kaizen activity with total participation, don't forget about the Kaizen after just doing it. **You have to write it down and make it visible—bring your Kaizen to the surface. It is absolutely necessary**.

118

Exercise for Kaizen Memo

"The creative person wants to be a know-it-all.
He wants to know about ancient history,
19th-century mathematics, manufacturing
techniques, flower arranging, and hog futures.
Because he never knows when these ideas
might come together to form a new idea."

Carl Ally

The good news is that writing down a Kaizen is extremely simple. A Kaizen can be written down in three minutes. What you need to do with Quick and Easy Kaizen is to write down the (1) Before Improvement, (2) After Improvement and (3) The Effect. Only those three points are needed. Of course, you can elaborate on those three points in great detail. But, as a whole, we don't want Kaizen to be written down in very great detail. If it is written down in great detail it takes time to read it. Kaizen, as we discussed, aims for shortcuts. Therefore, surfacing Kaizen should also aim for shortcuts.

3 report items:

- **Before: What was the problem?**
- **After: How was it improved?**
- **Effect: What were the results?**

Quick & Easy KAIZEN	
Before Improvement	*After Improvement*
The effect:	
Date:	**Name:**

The best method is to write each segment of the Kaizen report using as few words as necessary, maybe 25 words in total. But, Kaizen also says we shouldn't stick to one method. So we allow up to 75 words. We hope you will not exceed 75 words. Also if possible, include a picture, a drawing, or something visible.

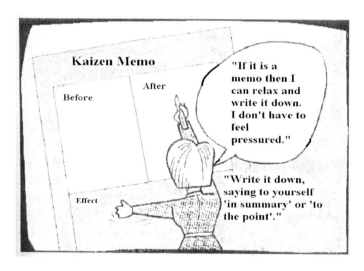

Quick and Easy Kaizen Memo.

Despite trying to persuade—even with a loud voice, many people still resist the idea that a Kaizen can be written down in

The Idea Generator – Quick and Easy Kaizen

three minutes. Most people fear that it is impossible, it cannot be done. They might say, "We have been implementing our improvement ideas and we do spend quite a lot of time on it. It is impossible to write it down in three minutes." Just listening to a lecture or reading this book, is not enough to convince people. To be convinced, you must experience it for yourself.

Understand it by doing it

So, the best thing is to try and actually do it or experience it, see whether it really can be done within three minutes and within 75 words. You will be convinced if you actually do it.

Scattered throughout the book and in the back of the book are a few blank Kaizen forms. We have asked you to think about some improvements that you or others have made in the last year and to write them down. The ideas could have been yours or from a fellow worker, or your boss or your subordinates—whatever Kaizens you have witnessed. Think about any small changes you have made in your work. Remember them and continue to write them down.

We want you to practice writing down Kaizens; it is essential for you to internalize the knowledge we present in this book. So please, stop reading for just a few minutes, and practice writing down at least one Kaizen right now. Thank you.

Quick & Easy KAIZEN	
Before Improvement	*After Improvement*
The effect:	
Date:	**Name:**

Some readers might think about, "Well, we changed the layout of some things the other day and the work flow became smoother." That could be a Kaizen. Look back six months or maybe one year. Think of how the work has been performed. There are many things you can think of to write down.

Kaizen could be some tangible material that has been changed or made, or intangible things that you have worked on. It doesn't have to be large. **Kaizen means small changes. Therefore, if it became a little bit easier, it became a little bit better,** that effect is fine.

For example, maybe the workplace developed a simple lookup card so that they have a quick and easy reference. Therefore, instead of checking from the very beginning, you can respond to a customer's inquiry more quickly with the card.

Or maybe it used to take much more time to calculate everything, but now you have a reference table. By looking at the table you don't have to add, but you can just transfer the figure from the table instead. Maybe that kind of Kaizen exists in your workplace. Or maybe, by using personal computers and installing a new program, calculation and analysis can be done immediately. Maybe you can think of some cases like that. There are a lot of Kaizens like that in the work place today. In the past you may have thought, "that's too small of a thing," or maybe thought "that's just common sense."

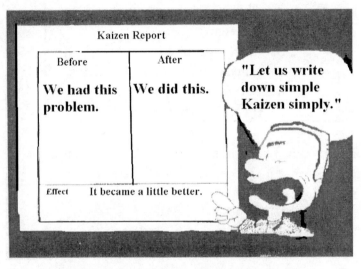

The meaning of Kaizen report (memo).

Think about those situations and write them down. We will help you with more exercises on how to quickly and easily write Kaizen memo in succeeding sections.

> **In summary**
> **To the point**
> **3 minutes**
> **75 words**

Exercise for Kaizen write up:
Write down two Kaizens in 6 minutes.

Some helpful tips…
1. **Think of a Kaizen from your own workplace or someone else's.**
2. **Think of an implemented Kaizen.**
3. **Start with pictures, illustrations, and drawings if it helps.**
4. **Use short sentences that are to the point or in summary.**

If you remember some additional Kaizens you already did in the past year, just jot them down for later discussion.

One Kaizen while Boiling a Three-minute Egg

*"Words are like eggs: when they
are hatched they have wings."*
Malagasy Proverb

If you are suddenly asked to write down your Kaizen without being given any time to think about it, you'll find you can do it very well. When we run our seminar and give attendees six minutes to write two Kaizens, we find that within five minutes many of them are already done and looking around. Sometimes we think that we should have asked them to do one more on another sheet. Exhibit 7-1 is an example.

Exhibit 7-1 Small Kaizen made by frontline worker

Before improvement:	After improvement:
Sometimes our hands burn when opening the black entrance door as black absorbs heat.	I painted the employee's entrance door with a lighter color so that when the sun shines on it all day it will reflect not absorb the heat.
Effect: The entrance door is now cooler and doesn't burn hands **Submitted By**: Sandra	

Kaizen can be written down very easily. There are some people, of course, who have only finished one Kaizen within the limited time. They are taking the time to remember what they have done and wonder which one to write down, things like that. Or, in other cases, they have too many Kaizen examples and are having difficulty making up their minds. Meanwhile, the time passes.

125

We are only concerned about 75 words that can easily be written down within three minutes. And we are not asking you to do multiple Kaizen examples every day. We are saying do at least one or two Kaizens per month, no matter how busy you are. Nobody would say they couldn't find two or three minutes of free time in their monthly work schedule.

Swiftly written down within 3 minutes!

Before
We had this problem.

After
We did this.

Effect
It became better.

Yes, you need only three minutes.

The implementation of Kaizen takes more time. Some can be done relatively easily, but in other cases you need to study or think about how it can be done, or it may require permission to begin.

Let us look at a number of different options:

1. You get an improvement idea and you write it down on the Kaizen form in the Before Improvement section.

Quick & Easy KAIZEN	
Before Improvement	**After Improvement**

2. Then you might check with your supervisor if you think that the idea will cost the company some money or might affect someone else. It is always good to check with someone else to get some feedback, support, or guidance on your idea.

3. You get an idea and test it on your own because it is a very simple change. Then you could show it to your supervisor after it works. If it doesn't work, then it doesn't hurt because it was so simple.

4. Your supervisor needs your help on a project such as how to improve customer service, and asks you to come up with ideas on what you think will please customers, like greeting them with a smile, or better ways of answering the customer's questions.

Kaizen is done before breakfast

To do something "before breakfast" is an expression that means it is very easy. So do Kaizen before the eggs are cooked.

Even though we say the implementation of Kaizen takes time, we do have enough time to do that. We have eight hours a day and we work more than 20 days per month. Simple Kaizen can be done very easily within that work schedule. The remaining task is simply to write it down in a memo format. If you have something to write about, the actual action of writing it down does not take much time.

If you place an egg in a pot of boiling water, it will be ready in three minutes. If you start writing a Kaizen memo when you add the egg to the pot, you will both be done at the same time. Maybe you only eat one three-minute egg per month. Fantastic! When you have that time, you can write a Kaizen down.

One written Kaizen before the egg is prepared

Once a month, review the way you do your job

During our seminars, we give people five or six minutes to write down two Kaizens. Five or six minutes can seem very short, but if you really concentrate it is quite long, too. That time allows you to remember many things and think about many things.

So, in this five or six minute exercise during the seminar, what did the participants think about and feel? Was it a waste of time to make this review? Or was it a time to review the way they do their jobs? It was a good opportunity to do that. Writing down Kaizens at least once a month encourages people to review their jobs at least once a month. This is a very healthful exercise.

Writing down a Kaizen once or twice a month is a chance for you to stop and review your own job. When you look back on your Kaizen accomplishments, it helps you to recognize your personal achievements, to share them with others and to make sure that the overall Kaizen process continues. Stopping at least once a month for a Kaizen review will help you improve your attitude toward your work. ***By surfacing your Kaizen through a Kaizen memo, you are institutionalizing that act of reviewing so that the Kaizen process will be sustained.***

> **Kaizen memo, one or two per month**
>
> **It is an opportunity to review your own work once a month**

However, if you are simply talking about reviewing your past improvement ideas once or twice every couple of months, it won't last long. You need a process of writing them down and sharing them to sustain this effort.

Also, if you look back at the number of Kaizen memos after one year, it becomes a reflection of how you have reviewed your work and how you studied your job each time and made changes.

"Looking into the future, innovation without improvement will lead us nowhere.

Improvement without innovation will sooner or later result in our demise.

We need constant innovation and improvement in a world of constant change to meet both our customers' perceptions and their expectations."

Akira Iwaki, CEO Iwaki Optical

Speak Short, Write Short, in 75 Words

*"Every composer knows the anguish and
despair occasioned by forgetting ideas
which one has not time to write down."*
Hector Berlioz

How can we write down a Kaizen using 75 words or less?

If you repeat the question above to yourself when you are writing, your sentences become very short. If you are approaching it like that, even though you may tend to write things in detail, you should not exceed more than 75 words if you keep saying to yourself "in summary" like that. By "summarizing it" from the start, your sentences will be compressed.

"To the point" or "in summary," repeating this is not only applicable to writing down Kaizen it is also a key in the workplace when you need to report something, communicate something, or to discuss something with somebody.

In many workplaces, there are people who are not good at summarizing or getting to the point while reporting, communicating, and discussing things. Since they go on and on, the listener inevitably asks, "What is your point?" Then they say, "There is an accident!" Then the person receiving the report feels like, "Why didn't you say so first!" These people are lacking the training to get to the point or to summarize.

For example, when people greeted with the question, "How are you?" some people elaborate and tell you all about their health problems their latest bout of the flu, an ulcer, or heaven forbid— their lumbago. But, "How are you?" is just a friendly way of greeting one another. And a simple "Fine" is a good answer. At another time, when appropriate, you can tell all about your problems.

"Make it short" is the phrase Lee Iococca, former CEO of Chrysler, used quite often. When the executives gave long-winded reports, he'd say, "Get to the point, make it short" and he often demanded this. "In summary" is another way of saying make it short. People who tend to add peripheral things, additional information, or excuses, often don't report the most important points until later. The Kaizen memo is *only* the most important points. Write it down, short.

When Iococca took over as CEO of Chrysler it went from facing bankruptcy to being restructured successfully in a short period of time. The management and Kaizen scale may be different, but the principle is the same. That is, make it short. Write it down short.

The Idea Generator – Quick and Easy Kaizen

"In a completely rational society, the best of us would aspire to be teachers and the rest of us would have to settle for something less, because passing civilization along from one generation to the next ought to be the highest honor and the highest responsibility anyone could have."
— **Lee Iococca**

Write Kaizen in a shortcut manner

When we say Kaizen should be written short, in short sentences, that also tends to invite argument. People who are against this, of course, tend to say, "Since this is a form we have to present to the company, it should be complete. It should be written down in detail so that everybody understands."

However, this type of thinking is behind the times. It doesn't fit with today's rapidly changing work environment or fast-paced jobs. What's more, it doesn't fit with Kaizen. If there is an official document, maybe lengthy details are necessary. But we are talking about a small Kaizen. Therefore, we don't have to make it that detailed. Kaizen should be written simply, in a shortcut manner. Let us give you one example:

Quick & Easy KAIZEN	
Before Improvement	After Improvement
We had this kind of problem	We took this corrective action
The effect: **We improved a little bit**	
Date:	Name:

When we see a complicated Kaizen report with many sentences, we might not want to read it—especially if we are pressed for time. We don't want Kaizen to be tedious for people, the easier for them the better. And the person who wrote the Kaizen report might not have felt good about it either. Many people are very self-conscious about their inability to express themselves in writing, and Kaizen should in no way make people feel threatened or uneasy. But we cannot blame someone for writing lengthy Kaizen memos either. Confusingly, many of our teachers taught us that more is better.

It is funny; one manager told me that he had a worker who wouldn't submit any ideas in writing. Now, he knew the worker was good at his job but absolutely refused to write down any Kaizen ideas. A light bulb went off and one day this manager finally realized that the worker could not read nor write. So he carefully told the worker, "Hey, Jack that was a very good idea that you had about fixing that machine problem, can you do me a favor and let me write down the idea and submit it. It will be very valuable for others to see it."

The Idea Generator – Quick and Easy Kaizen

If you actually take the time to read the following Kaizen, the content of the Kaizen is very good. But when it is written down in a very detailed manner like that it doesn't communicate it well.

Quick & Easy KAIZEN	
Before Improvement	**After Improvement**
My workplace is outside of the company and I have to travel on my motorcycle. When it rains, water drops hit my helmet and it makes it very difficult for me to see through the helmet. Since I can't see very well, it makes it very dangerous for me to ride in the rain. But, I have to make my deliveries on time so I am always fearful of falling and hurting myself and the motorcycle.	I came up with the idea to apply rain resistant chemicals, which are sold in the auto shops, and apply that to the mask of my helmet. The chemicals can be applied easily before I go out into the rain on my motorcycle.
Effect: So, by applying that, the water drops run off of the mask and it is easy to see. It became much safer.	
Date: 08-16-2000 Name: Harry Smith	

If you ask someone to get to the point, then you can convert this Kaizen report like this:

Quick & Easy KAIZEN	
Before Improvement	**After Improvement**
It was difficult to see in the rain because water stuck to my mask of my helmet.	I applied silicon to the surface of the mask.
Effect: The water drops scatter because of the water repellent and it is easier to see. Therefore it is safer to drive.	

Writing directly and to the point, we wrote this memo using 47 words. We probably could have done it with fewer words, too.

Compare the two reports. Which is easier to read and which is easier to understand? Which report do you want to read? The first report is so detailed and difficult to understand and read. You want the Kaizen memo to be simple, easy to read and understand.

The purpose of the Kaizen report is to show exactly what you did to address a problem, your solution and the results obtained. The report is used to share this information with others to stimulate them to make similar improvements with their work.

Some companies do give small rewards for Kaizens that are implemented. At one Dana plant, the idea reports are placed into a barrel and each quarter a number of Kaizen reports are pulled out of the barrel for large prizes. At other companies, each person submitting an implemented Kaizen receives maybe a dollar, five dollars—and some could receive up to $100 for an important idea.

Kaizen should be written down as if you are jotting down a memo.

The Idea Generator – Quick and Easy Kaizen

Kaizen should be written down in short, simple, concise sentences. We are not talking about a document to be presented to a government office. We are talking about a Kaizen memo. When we use the term "Kaizen report," it sounds like a stiff expression and may make people feel like they have to be stiff too.

To avoid this situation, most companies have changed the name from Kaizen report to Kaizen memo, as we will now refer to it in this book. Also, if you start writing your Kaizens in a memo format, you can compile those memos to build a collection of simple Kaizens. By using that compilation as a reference, you could help to stimulate others and use those as a hinge for further improvement.

If it is Understood, Then it is Fine

"Nothing in life is to be feared.
It is only to be understood."
Marie Curie

You may find it easier to get started writing down a Kaizen if you begin with an illustration or picture first. What did you do? How did you do it? What happened? Those are the points to be communicated. If someone understands that by looking at the illustration, that's all you need. You don't have to write down unnecessary things. In short, if it is understandable it is fine.

3 points:

- **What did you do?**
- **How did you do it?**
- **What happened?**

Of course, depending on the type of job or the content of the Kaizen, it may not be understood through an illustration alone. If so, then you can add sentences. The sentences are just supplemental. Therefore, you can just add a minimum amount of sentences to the illustration. When you write a sentence, the best way to do this is to repeat to yourself:

- **In summary, what did I do?**
- **In summary, how did I do it?**
- **In summary, what happened?**

Exhibit 7-2 In summary for 90 degree fixture rotation

Before improvement:	After improvement:
Difficult to rotate fixture 90 degrees	Added two tapped holes to spindle press
Effect: Easy now to rotate the fixture 90 degree	
Submitted By: Ken	

Exhibit 7-2 is a typical case of a short Kaizen memo. OK. Now we will give you six minutes. Please write down two separate Kaizens using the forms below.

Quick & Easy KAIZEN	
Before Improvement	**After Improvement**
The effect:	
Date:	**Name:**

Quick & Easy KAIZEN	
Before Improvement	**After Improvement**
The effect:	
Date:	**Name:**

When we teach this in a seminar format, the participants feel pressed for time during the six minute / two Kaizen exercise, so we use music in the background to relax them.   After five minutes have passed, we ask the participants who have already finished their two Kaizens to count the number of words they have used. We notice that most people start counting the words on their paper. This tells us that most participants in five minutes have already done their two Kaizen reports.   Then afterward, when we check, most people have also written their Kaizens in fewer than 75 words. Those who haven't tried the exercise will continue to think that it is difficult to write two Kaizen reports in six minutes. To help you recognize your own ability, we ask that if you haven't done it yet, please stop reading now and complete those two Kaizen reports!

After we finish this six-minute exercise in our seminar, we say, "If you have written down two complete Kaizens, please raise your hand."   Usually, 80% of the participants raise their hands.

The Idea Generator – Quick and Easy Kaizen

Then, we say, "OK, now we have a 10 minute break. Those people who started to write their second Kaizen can use this break to finish it up." We hope you were able to finish your two Kaizens in your six minutes, but if not, go ahead and finish writing them now.

Simple Kaizens should be written simply. If a simple Kaizen is written down in detail, it is difficult for others to understand what it is. If the Kaizen is exceptionally big, as an exception you can write it in greater detail. But that is the exception.

Kaizen documentation Q & A

Here are some questions we are frequently asked about the Kaizen memo system, followed by our answers.

Q: If a Kaizen memo is so brief, other people might not always understand. Shouldn't Kaizen be written in more detail so that anybody can understand?

A: A simple Kaizen should be written down simply. If a simple Kaizen is described in detail, it becomes confusing. The idea that writing in greater detail is better is a misconception. When something is too detailed, it becomes harder to under stand. By "padding" the information, the most important points become lost in the other information. Therefore, the

141

main point of your Kaizen becomes unclear. In fact, the purpose of Kaizen documentation or surfacing Kaizen ideas is not to report the details of the Kaizen. All we are concerned with is what was the problem, what did you do, and what happened. If you compare the detailed Kaizen report with a simple Kaizen memo, you understand this immediately. If you try to elaborate on things that can be understood more easily; you can make it too complicated and end up in confusion.

Q: We want to protect our ISO certification, and if workers are allowed to continuously make changes then how can we control our standards?

A: Of course you want to control your standards. You want to make sure that procedures are adhered to and that the output quality is rigorously maintained. First, you will find that 90% of the implemented ideas will not affect your standards, for they are very small changes, as you can see from many of the examples in this book. Second, if the improvements help make the company more competitive, you may *want* to change your standards. If you develop a better "light bulb," you don't want to stop the progress of your company by not producing the new "light bulb" just to maintain your standards. If there is a better way to do something then you should do it. You must exercise care, of course, that quality is maintained and that people are properly trained with the new procedure. However, the ISO standard was not designed to restrict progress at all.

Quick & Easy KAIZEN	
Before Improvement	**After Improvement**
The effect:	
Date:	**Name:**

The Kaizen Report as a Confession

"I am not ashamed to confess
I am ignorant of what I do not know."
Marcus Tullius Cicero

With Kaizen Examples, Look at the Reality Squarely

A Kaizen memo, which states what a worker has done, is in a way a confession. After all, if the Kaizen memo says, "I improved something," it also means, "I was doing something wrong before." And depending on the Kaizen, it might even suggest that someone was doing 'stupid' things before. After all, if you were doing wonderfully well, there would be no need for Kaizen, right? But since you've been doing things that do have room for improvement, you have room for Kaizen. But oh, dear, if you have many Kaizen memos, that means lots of things weren't going that well, doesn't it? In other words, by practicing Quick and Easy Kaizen, you are admitting and confessing to being imperfect, maybe even confessing that you were doing stupid things!

Why then encourage that kind of confession through the Kaizen memo?

To succeed today in this very competitive world requires everyone to do their part in making improvements, to reduce costs, to improve quality, to improve safety, to improve customer service, and to eliminate every possible waste. Even though the Kaizen memo can be temporarily embarrassing as it reveals to others that we have been making mistakes, It is far

better to be temporarily embarrassed than to continue to make the same mistakes over and over again.

Also, please understand we're not saying that because many companies are doing it, you should be doing it too. That is nonsense. What other companies do has nothing to do with what you should be doing. Your company should do what is good for your company. You should think about what is beneficial to you and to your company. And if what you're currently doing is not, stop doing it.

I don't know about you but I have done a lot of things incorrectly in my life. You might even call them 'stupid' things. And I am very happy that I have learned from doing those things and stopped doing them. When I was young I couldn't even tie my shoes correctly, but with my parents patience I learned how. I also remember when I was 19, I was trying to show off to a girl I recently met. I felt so good at the time that I attempted to do a handstand on top of an old wooden fence. Trouble was that I'd never done a handstand on the ground, let alone on top of a wooden fence. The result? The fence collapsed and I ended up in the hospital with torn cartilage in my left knee.

Sometimes it takes a while to learn lessons properly. A year later, I tried to show off again with a new date that I really liked. I picked her up to carry her up some steps and dropped her. That was the end of that relationship.

Even a few years ago I was on a wonderful bicycle ride, going very fast on Martha's Vineyard on a beautiful summer day. I felt like the wind. I thought I was Greg Lemond, the winner of the

French Tour d'France. I was traveling on a bicycle at 35 miles an hour, alone on this peaceful lovely day, when a truck appeared in the middle of the road. Next thing I knew I was on the ground, totally stunned, with a broken hip. It took me three months to learn how to walk again.

I have more than enough 'stupid' examples of the mistakes I have made in life. I could probably write another dozen books about them. I hope now that I am co-writing this book with Bunji Tozawa, I can begin to look carefully around and make my Kaizens a real habit—and substantially reduce the mistakes and stupid things I do!

Summary

1. Complaints heard often: The Kaizen has already been done. I don't like to write it down. It is cumbersome to write it down. Why do you need to write Kaizen down?

2. Please write down your Kaizens because otherwise some people will do it:

   • **Partially**
   • **Temporarily**
   • **Sporadically**

3. You want to bring Kaizen to the surface:

   • **Consciously**
   • **Continuously**
   • **Through total participation**

4. To succeed with a Quick and Easy Kaizen system it is
    absolutely necessary to write the Kaizens down and make
    them visible for others to see.

Quick & Easy KAIZEN	
Before Improvement	**After Improvement**
The effect:	
Date:	Name:

5. A Kaizen memo can be written down in three minutes.
    One Kaizen can be written down while you are waiting for
    your three-minute eggs to boil.

6. Although the Kaizen memo is simple, by making it visible
    you can actually see your progress, and it makes it
    possible to sustain that activity.

7. You only need write one or two Kaizen memos per month.
    It is an opportunity to review your own work once a
    month.

8. Say it short. Write it short.

9. To do that, the phrase you should use is "in summary." In summary, what was the problem? In summary, what did you do? In summary, what happened?

Quick & Easy KAIZEN	
Before Improvement	**After Improvement**
The effect:	
Date:	Name:

Quick & Easy KAIZEN	
Before Improvement	**After Improvement**
The effect:	
Date:	Name:

Chapter 8: Visualization and Inspection

*"The things we have to learn before we
can do them, we learn by doing them."*
Aristotle

**Instead of saying, "be careful," change your methods so that
you don't have to be careful.**

Let us now study the steps, principles or rules of Kaizen. The most fundamental principle of Kaizen is to visualize things. We want to visualize those things you cannot normally see.

One way to do this visualization is to imagine that you are like a general in the Army inspecting his troops. You prepare an improvement checklist in advance, something that you will add to as you inspect and learn, and you go out and inspect your work area. As you look closely with your new inspection list you will begin to see things in a whole new way.

As I mentioned earlier in the book, I once took a camera and visited local drug stores in my area. I looked first at the front of the store to see how inviting it was to enter. I then looked at the entranceway, the floors, ceilings, doorways, and shelves, around the cash registers, around the pharmaceutical department, the storage areas and even the bathroom. I looked at the way the employees were dressed and how they looked at their customers. I took pictures of everything.

I found a mountain of things that could be improved. Shelves were in disarray, boxes and supplies all over the floors, ceilings were water damaged and dirty, doorways were broken, and many of the walls needed painting. Once again I did the same thing with my own work area. I took pictures of my desk, my shelves, and my files and found numerous improvement ideas for me to work on in my personal Kaizen-a-day improvement campaign.

I love taking pictures for its simple but very powerful function. I recommend that you take pictures throughout the work area of your company. Then post the pictures on the wall or a bulletin board and ask your employees to come up with improvement ideas. Continue to take a picture of the same work area once a month and review the progress with your employees. You can even pick themes for improvement, like safety or housekeeping or visual control. You will be amazed at the improvements and, of course, I recommend that you praise your employees for their achievements. Visualization can be used in many ways to make improvements.

Turning off the switches

Many workplaces have problems like forgetting to turn off switches. For instance, like turning off the air-conditioning switch. In those places, which do not do Kaizen very well, there are people who might say, "just be careful" for the forgetfulness or mistakes. "Be careful! Do it right!" those people cry and yell like that. But the truth is, these problems cannot be solved by just saying "be careful," "be mindful," and so forth.

Non-Kaizen promoted workplace

Naturally, right after somebody says "be careful," people will be more mindful to make sure to check whether they have turned off the switch and so forth. And maybe they will do it over and over again to be sure. However, this kind of attention doesn't last long. They will soon become more relaxed and this is followed by another forgetful mistake.

People have been scolded for forgetting, but somehow the scolding doesn't always work and people still forget. Then you might tell them "well we have to have people do a thorough job." "Be thorough. Make sure." Those words are repeated often, and frankly they're overused. Workplaces where you often hear the word "thorough" used, are often not doing thorough jobs—that's why they must say "Be thorough!" And just saying those words does not change their way of doing things. Unless you change the method, the way you do your job, the same mistake will be done repeatedly; the same problem will continue repeating itself over and over again.

My grandson's Nicholas age 14 and Douglas age 11 recently spent a week with me in the Portland area. I would tell Douglas to

151

be careful walking a cross the street and he would immediately do the opposite and not look. I then thought of changing the method. Instead of telling Douglas to be careful I explained the problem and asked him to come up with a way to be careful crossing the street. He said, "I should look both ways and if a one way street I should still look both ways but especially in the direction where the traffic is coming."

On the other hand, in a workplace with Kaizen they do not use those statements in vain, over and over. They will talk about things like "Let's change, so we don't have to be careful. Let's change so that we can do a thorough job." If these places have trouble, for example, remembering to turn off the air-conditioning switch, they say, "Let us devise a way so that we cannot forget turning off the switch, even if we are not mindful."

Dr. W. Edwards Deming, the great quality guru, in his famous fourteen points[*] stated that you should, "Eliminate slogans, exhortations, and targets for the workforce asking for zero defects and new levels of productivity. Such exhortations only create adversarial relationships, as the bulk of the causes of low quality and low productivity belong to the system and thus lie beyond the power of the workforce."

He also said to, "Remove barriers that rob the hourly worker of his/her right to pride of workmanship. The responsibility of supervisors must be changed from sheer numbers to quality."

We think both points make a solid case for installing a Quick and Easy Kaizen system to foster creative involvement from all employees. Rather than just using words to cajole people to im-

---

[*] See http://caes.mit.edu/deming/14-points.html for the fourteen points.

prove, you challenge them to come up with their own small ideas to insure that mistakes and problems are eliminated. **You let the worker become a real partner in the improvement process.**

Let us install a Kaizen so that we won't forget.

Here is just one example of using the visualizing technique to change the method regarding things you cannot normally see: in this case, the flow of air. Simply put a ribbon at the air outlet of the air-conditioning machine. By doing that, when the air comes out from that outlet, the ribbon will be waving so that, at a glance, workers know whether the switch is on or not. If it is still on, from a distance you can see it. Therefore it is easier no longer easy to forget.

Exhibit 8-1 Kaizen report for turning off the switches (1)

Before Improvement	After Improvement
Remember to check the switch of the air-conditioner.	The ribbon shows the airflow at a glance.

The Effect: At a glance, we can confirm whether the switch is on or off.

The reason why that switch was always forgotten is because in the past it was not easy to notice whether the switch was on or off at a glance in the distance. They had a little small light, but it was hidden and very difficult to see. Of course, there are many ways to improve that situation. Since the light is too small, you can make a bigger light. But for this example you have to use a bigger light and it will consume some electricity all the time. And moreover, you have to have special wiring to make that connection. Therefore, that idea costs a little more money and is more cumbersome. But the simple idea of just adding a ribbon is very easy and effective. This is a great example of Quick and Easy Kaizen.

Kaizen is often just a simple shift, but even very small changes can be very effective.

This idea can be applied not just with air-conditioning but wherever you have airflow, for example a fan or cooling system. When the fan is not working continuously, overheating can occur inside the machine. To prevent that from happening you might want to see, visually, whether the fan is working or not. There are many ways to make that happen. The simplest method would be the same way, just putting a ribbon where the air comes out.

Exhibit 8-2 Kaizen report for turning off the switches (2)

Before Improvement	After Improvement
This machine has a cooling fan inside. Sometimes the cooling fan does not work and it overheats.	Putting a ribbon in front of the fan.

OK!

The Effect: The airflow can be seen all the time.

The Idea Generator – Quick and Easy Kaizen

When we visited another plant, we saw many pinwheels like you can buy at festivals. So we asked what they are for. They explained that when the fan in the machine is working this wheel turns. Therefore, we can detect the condition of the inside of the machine's airflow. Of course, here they could use a ribbon too. But to make it more interesting, you can sometimes use a ribbon or sometimes you might want to have some variety by using a pinwheel, whatever you think would be most effective in the particular situation. This is another example of visualization.

Changing the shape of the faucet

The air and wind are not the only things you can't see; you also cannot see water or liquid inside a pipe or hose. In one plant we visited, there was a tank of warm water, and there was a hose connecting the tank to where they could add water for adjustment of the temperature. However, they had the problem of being forgetful about the water flow. This problem also cannot be solved by saying, "be careful." This requires a Kaizen, a change in method. First, you might look carefully at the faucet and try to visualize what improvements can be made. For this particular type of control, you could not detect at a glance whether the faucet was open or closed. So, they changed the knob to a lever.

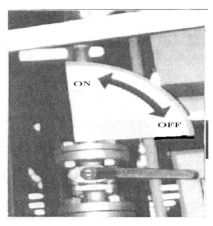

Picture of the lever with two-way arrow

Now you can easily see at a glance whether it is opened or closed. If the lever is parallel to the pipe, then it is opened fully. When it is at an angle to the pipe, then it is closed. If it is diagonal, then it is half-opened and half-closed. This is an example of making the flow of the water inside the pipe visible by changing the knob to a lever. The lever shows how much flow of water is going on inside the pipe.

The question to ask ourselves when we have problems with invisible things is: "What can we do to make it visible?" If you want to see things more clearly inside a pipe, then maybe you can change the situation by using something that makes a noise inside the pipe when the water flows, or use translucent pipe that you can see inside of. Explore the possibilities.

The Idea Generator – Quick and Easy Kaizen

Exhibit 8-3 Kaizen report for detecting water level

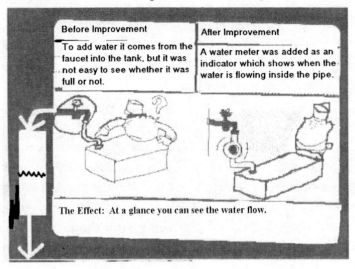

Before Improvement	After Improvement
To add water it comes from the faucet into the tank, but it was not easy to see whether it was full or not.	A water meter was added as an indicator which shows when the water is flowing inside the pipe.

The Effect: At a glance you can see the water flow.

Inspection of Your Work

"As long as one keeps searching,
the answers come."
Joan Baez

Surfacing Kaizen actually is the review of your own work, or you may say a periodical check. It is a system to allow you to review your own job on a regular basis. Without that kind of system, you may be too busy to look back or review the way you do your job because you are constantly racing with the task you have at hand. You are used to thinking you have to finish what is in front of you first.

Maybe that kind of situation was okay in the past, where changes were not that significant. And maybe in the past people around you might have said, "You don't need to do anything extra. Just do what you are told to do," or something like that. But today things are changing rapidly. New technology, new materials are introduced constantly. Things you did in the past might not be necessary today. Or today you can do many of the same things much more easily and simply. If you don't notice those changes, then you just say, "We have been doing this all along, we have been told to do it this way," and you just keep it the way it has always been.

If improvements are to take place, it really is necessary to review your way of doing your job at least once a month by asking these questions:

- **Do we really need to do this to this extent?**

The Idea Generator – Quick and Easy Kaizen

- **Is it possible to stop doing this?**

The act of surfacing Kaizen once a month is really a warning, or perhaps a reminder. **Don't stick to only one way. Look around; there might be a better method.** Maybe we are the only ones still doing it like this and the other companies have found new ways. And maybe this will also encourage you to look around, ask other people, study, copy ideas from others, and things like that.

Mere talking is not good enough

Some of you will be able to take the information in this book and begin to teach others in your company Quick and Easy Kaizen. Others may want to read the book one chapter at a time with team members and then begin to experiment together, while some of you might also want to participate in a seminar.[*]

Most often when we read, we do not take the words directly from the book and begin experimenting with the new knowledge. Just reading is limited. You must also practice Kaizen. We do encourage you to review your work and start to write up Kaizen memos as you read this book and begin to share them with your fellow workers.

---

[*] If interested in an in-house seminar please e-mail me at seminar@pcspress.com

159

I made some changes!

Just reading or talking about Kaizen will not improve your workplace, so make sure that you have reviewed your work and written a Kaizen each month. What have you reviewed and what was the result? Have you been doing anything inefficiently? If so, what? Have you stopped doing it? Have you reduced something? Have you changed something? You should be tracking Kaizens to that extent. If you have changed something, what did you change and in what way? Tell me about that. You have to ask people to talk about their changes, to document them and share with the others. If you don't ask them this way, if you just ask them to "review," it won't work.

Some people will inevitably say, "Yes, I did review my work. I didn't find any problems at all." Maybe that is all you can expect. For just reading this book might not cause you to start making changes.

As we've discussed, the report doesn't have to be in detail. A brief memo is enough for Kaizen. Remember, **Kaizen results do not last without surfacing the ideas for others to see.** That's the reason. Temporarily, your change might have people excited, but it will not continue that way without regular documentation. After training people, you might find that only a few of them continue to practice making Kaizens. You might find that sooner or later they stop doing Kaizen. It is very hard to break past habits and start doing new things.[*]

The reason for that is that Kaizen is a kind of rebellion. If you think about it, Kaizen is a challenge to your predecessor who told you to do it the old way. You are challenging that notion. Maybe it is no longer necessary to do that, or perhaps you have found a more effective way to do it, a more efficient way. Maybe the past method that we learned is obsolete. So you are really challenging the past.

> # Kaizen is a rebellion against the past!

In the past, that type of rebelliousness was not appreciated in the workplace. Managers would tell the workers "Don't argue. Don't do anything extra. Just do what I have told you," and things like that. But whether you like it or not, the world is changing. Hardheaded people have to recognize that fact. "That is right. Exactly, as you say. Well, the method you are suggesting does seem easier." In that way, they have to recognize the shortcomings of the past.

This past summer while on vacation with my grandsons I was sitting at the table at a Bread and Breakfast in San Juan Island speaking with a professor from Virginia. When I told him I was

---

[*] Try to apply Quick and Easy Kaizen to changing your habits – take some small steps and see the magic happen.

161

writing a book about getting ideas from all workers, he told me that once he offered ideas to his department head but the chairperson felt that it was criticism of his job. The professor stopped offering further improvement ideas. We must change that kind of attitude through Quick and Easy Kaizen. We must show supervision the necessity, the vital necessity, to allow everyone to be involved in making improvements. Isn't it ironical that the attitude even exists at a college level?

We are the creatures of emotion. We understand changes and the need to change, but emotionally sometimes we have the resistance to that. Although, as a senior-level employee, you understand the need for change. But what if the newcomers come in and say, "Here is a better way; this is more efficient"? How does that make the bosses or senior people feel? They may say, "Well, the young people have a good point" or something like that. They may say that on the surface, but deep down they are not so easily persuaded.

If I stop and look back at myself, I can see a life filled with both change and vast resistance to change. After two years in the army, I started my professional career as an accountant working for carpenters in the East Bronx. I would sit in their shops wearing a suit and a tie and covered with sawdust, with no air conditioning in the summer and very little heat in the winter. I was struggling to barely make a living. But, I was truly blessed with a desire to grow and to change. Change was always difficult, always challenging, often even painful, but the result in the long run was always wonderful. It's like Arnold Schwarzenegger once said, "No pain, no gain." In other words, growth doesn't come easily, but it is surely worth the effort.

You need the support of the boss!

Unless the boss fully and positively supports the Kaizen activity, it will simply disappear. If the boss shows signs of being upset or gives a nasty comment or something like that, those people who have been doing Kaizen passionately in the beginning will, of course, feel it is not worth continuing Kaizen. Most people who have experienced this begin to say, "I understand. I no longer do anything beyond my duty. I do what I was told to do, and that only" and things like that. In this unfortunate situation, both the company and the individual loses. In better economic times, we might suggest that the worker immediately go and find another job with another company, one that respects the "rights" of people to be heard creatively.

Ask the worker

The best way to make improvements is to ask the worker to help. Ask the worker to come up with Kaizens. **The worker is the real expert; he or she knows the job the best.** After all, it is the worker who is doing the job every day.

The people that continue to install many Kaizens, enthusiastically risk being called eccentrics. They have broken the mold, and continue to. In some companies a polarization takes place between groups of people who do Kaizen and groups of people who do not do Kaizen. And this polarization tends to grow more in the larger companies and the companies with the longer histories.

Employee's fears about doing Kaizen.

Many people feel that the easiest way to get along in the workplace is to do only what you have been told to do. If you don't have to think about it or judge it, then all you need to do is perform it out of habit. Come to work, do your work in the same manner, and go back home again. What happens when all of your employees do that and nothing more? The company loses its vitality. The company becomes a group of people with no energy or motivation and you start to lose your customers.

In that kind of situation, no company will be able to meet the changing world. They will be left behind the times. Those people who manage and lead that organization need to take countermeasures.

I once saw a person working in front of a punch press. He would take his left hand and pick up a piece of sheet metal and place the sheet into the punch press. He would then activate the punch press by placing both his hands onto buttons outside of the press. This procedure of using both hands was a safety precaution to prevent him from accidentally crushing his hands in the press. After the punch press formed the sheet metal into a part, he would reach in with his right hand to remove the part.

I turned to his manager and asked, "How many plates will he do in a day?" His answer was, "5,000." "How many did he do yesterday? "5,000." How many will he do tomorrow? "5,000."

I do not blame the worker for doing the same job every day. He has to make a living, and he does not have the power to change that easily. It is up to the manager to offer opportunities for em-ployees to grow and change jobs, or to challenge them with Quick and Easy Kaizen so that they have the opportunity to make their jobs more interesting.

Probably with some simple engineering the plates could have been loaded into and removed from the punch press automatically. The operator then could have been given more challenging work.

On that note, I visited one plant many years ago that allowed workers to change jobs at the end of every week. Workers could post their jobs onto a bulletin board and weekly switch them with other workers. This allowed them to build their skills and meet new challenges in the work place.

If you don't do anything, the employees just maintain the status quo. How can we encourage them to tackle their jobs in a more positive manner? One countermeasure for that is to write a Kaizen down after you have done it, not just stopping after implementation. In other words, surfacing Kaizen.

Whenever, I get an idea for an improvement, I immediately put it on my Kaizen "to do" list. Then I make a concerted effort to do it. I try to do at least one every week. Since I am making only small changes, I am able to get started on items right away.

We ask people to write down their Kaizen implementations. By doing that, you can develop a simple Kaizen list or compilation of Kaizen examples, and by looking at a booklet with examples, people will be relieved to say, "Well, if that kind of Kaizen is okay, I can do that too. There are many similar things I can do." It will affect those people who previously thought Kaizen was really difficult or that Kaizen is beyond them. They can say, "Well, if that was okay then I can do it too" and adopt that kind of attitude.

The most important thing in Kaizen activity to be able to teach others is to have your own Kaizen examples, at least ten of them.

The Japan Human Resource Association in Tokyo has been publishing a magazine called *Creativity and Ingenuity* for 20 years. This small magazine includes many Kaizen examples from different industries and different types of jobs every month, month after month. Since they have already published more than 200 issues, they have lots and lots of examples.

The Idea Generator – Quick and Easy Kaizen

People who understand Kaizen well can look at other companies' examples in this magazine and understand the way they have changed. They can take that information and say, "I can really learn something from this. I can apply this to my Kaizen next time."

But in any company, you cannot expect everybody to be that open-minded and able to understand, even though you present excellent Kaizen examples. Some people will refuse to buy in and say, "This Kaizen is fine, but that is a different industry. We are talking about different sizes of organizations. We have a different type of job." For those people, showing examples of other companies obviously won't work.

To convince those people, the examples will have to come from their own company, their own workplace, actual examples will need to be used. This is where your own Kaizen memos can be of use.

Will Kaizen Reduce the Workforce?

"The sad truth is that excellence
makes people nervous."
Shana Alexander

By developing and sharing your own workplace Kaizen examples, we can avoid unnecessary, unproductive discussion or confusion about Kaizen.

Some people might argue, "The reason why companies are discussing Kaizen activity in the midst of a sluggish economy is because they want to reduce the workforce." And if Kaizen is poorly introduced to the workplace, workers themselves might think, "Because the company is suffering due to poor business conditions, they want to restructure. Therefore they push Kaizen. If we cooperate, workers like us are harming ourselves."

This kind of thinking can happen when people use the word "efficiency" instead of "improvement," i.e. "Well, if we improve our jobs and our work becomes more efficient, and it took ten people to do the job the old way, but now we can do it with nine... that means one person gets laid-off." Listening to this is very convincing. Other people react and say, "That is right. Think about it. If we do Kaizen too much somebody might get laid-off. And the next time it could be me. I am AGAINST KAIZEN!"

This is the time you really need the specific Kaizen examples. By showing specific Kaizen examples, it is obvious that this amount of Kaizen is not going to reduce the workforce. These are small changes. Therefore the extent of the effect is to make things

168

go a little easier, a little smoother, to reduce some of the frustration at work. For example, if getting the air conditioning switch turned off is a problem, then attaching the ribbon to the air outlet can solve that problem. No matter how many ribbons you attach, it is probably not going to reduce the workforce. It is improbable that this type of Kaizen will ever result in workforce reduction.

Small-change Quick and Easy Kaizen does not have the power to reduce the workforce. The only effect it has is a little bit of waste reduction, a little bit of speeding things up, a little bit of reducing forgetfulness and mistakes.

If you look at specific examples, it becomes obvious. If you make sure to discuss Kaizen with specific examples in your own workplace, you can avoid the meaningless discussion of whether Kaizen will reduce the workforce or not. With good Kaizen examples, the discussion becomes very simple; people can see at a glance that Kaizen will not reduce the workforce.

Also, most companies that have a successful Quick and Easy Kaizen system make a commitment up front that a worker will not lose his job due to their improvement activities. If they end up with extra people, then they will make new investments to build new products or create new services.

Every day it is good to focus a little on change and improvement. The world surely needs improvement in many respects and so do most people. Yet it is challenging to make changes in life. Fundamentally, though, life is really about growing—and that brings success on every level. You gain new skills, you gain knowledge, you gain more experience, and you learn how to serve others better. Everyone needs a little push to make changes. Kaizen will help make that push.

Kaizen is Profitable or Not Profitable, Gain or Loss

*"It is a profitable thing, if one is
wise, to seem foolish."*
Aeschylus

There are people in the company who will have difficulty understanding this point about Kaizen being profitable or not profitable, a gain or a loss for the employee. But it is important for all these people to understand what Kaizen is. For these people, we have to show some examples, like the one on the next page.

Since you are working in the company and get paid, you have to accomplish the tasks you are given. Let's say your task is to carry a stone. If you don't think about an easier way to carry it, you may need to continuously do it with the same old method. Or, to the extent that you can within your workplace, you can change the method to make it easier. What is beneficial to you, yourself? What is easier? What is safer? What is more comfortable? **In other words, what is the gain for you?**

Be careful though; if you try to discuss this in terms of which is "right or wrong" for an employee, then people have different views and will inevitably argue. They might say, "Well, if you are suffering, it contributes to your growth and it is better for you." Or maybe someone would even say, "The more difficult way is a beneficial way, for it gives you a physical work-out!" However, the company is not an exercise gym. Nor is it the place for boot camp-style training for your physical strength. It's a place to do your job.

The Idea Generator – Quick and Easy Kaizen

As well, since people's taste and values are different, talking about it in terms of good/bad or likes/dislikes could also become very confusing. So, simply asking whether this improvement is to your benefit, is it to your gain or loss, is most understandable. If there are still people who have difficulty understanding this point, show them examples of improvements and then simply ask them if it easier or better for them.

In that case, it is also important for you to have examples specific to that person's job to help share what Kaizen means. If the person does office work, show examples of office work Kaizen. By looking at it this way, it becomes obvious that Kaizen means to change the cumbersome way of doing work to make it simpler and easier. And by comparing those examples it becomes understandable which is a gain and which is a loss to the individual.

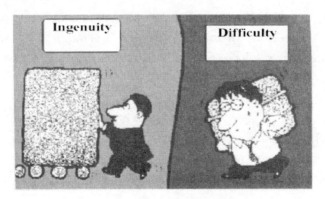

You can reduce your suffering.

There are different ways of moving this rock, like either carrying it or pushing it. Don't stick to only one way of doing the work. Devise a way so that you can use shortcuts with good results. Use Kaizen to select the proper means to do a job more efficiently or change the methods to do the job more efficiently. With Kaizen, you can change yourself and you can change your workplace.

> **Don't stick to one way of doing the work.**
>
> **With Kaizen you can change yourself and you can change your workplace.**

Once, many years ago I was extremely troubled about the state of the world. I wanted to do something, but I didn't know what to do. I was studying with a teacher, Rudi, who pulled me aside and said, "Norman, you are trying to save the world and you can't even save yourself. Stop trying to help the world and begin to work on yourself. You work on yourself and improve and then you will see that the world will become a better place. After you have worked on yourself for 15 years, then you can go out and help others and help the world."

I am very grateful that I took his advice and really started to work very hard on myself. And I think that today I am a better person with fewer tensions, and I am more capable of helping someone else improve.

Change: Method
       View point
       Thoughts

With Kaizen you can change yourself.

In a sense, you don't really have to do Kaizen for the company's benefit. You can just be concerned with your own benefit. And **Kaizen should be done to benefit you.** You should clearly state this. **The person who gains the most from the Kaizen is the person who did the Kaizen.** Kaizen is not only for the company's sake. By looking at Kaizen examples, people realize that Kaizen is beneficial to them and that it is very good for them personally.

> **The person who gains the most from the Kaizen is the person who did the Kaizen.**

Of course, if each individual aims to improve his or her work and to accomplish the work objectives so they can do a better job, make the workplace safer and more comfortable, the whole company would benefit through improved productivity and a better bottom line. That is the reason a company would create a Kaizen activity system and reward employees for their Kaizen efforts; in the end the company will benefit. But for the company's sake, the primary purpose of Kaizen is for the employee's own benefit. It should begin as a benefit for each individual.

In other words, if your Kaizen doesn't benefit you, it is not Kaizen. If it benefits you, or your fellow employee it is Kaizen.

Everyone wants to do a good job. If people begin to look around them and are encouraged to improve the way their job is done, they will feel better about their work and themselves.

Kaizen doesn't expect self-sacrificing devotion to the company for the company's benefit and things like that. If you do Kaizen for your own benefit, as a result it may benefit the company also. That should be the way. However, when managers and bosses say, "Do Kaizen for your own sake!" some employees think it is too good to be true. They doubt their boss's sincerity. "For our own benefit? Maybe they are just saying that to make us happy," think the employees. Some people cannot simply accept it!

When management is confronted with these objections it is another good time to use specific Kaizen examples. Those people

The Idea Generator – Quick and Easy Kaizen

who cannot believe what the managers say might change their opinion when they see specific examples. Show them the Kaizen examples so that they can see who is really benefiting. Is that Kaizen beneficial to that individual or are they losing something? By looking at the Kaizen examples, it is easy to understand that. When a discussion is based on the Kaizen examples it goes a lot more smoothly. There is no room for unnecessary, unproductive discussion. This is a great and important effect of using specific examples.

Summary

1. **Improvement by visualization includes:**

    *   **Displaying, indication and signs**
    *   **Emphasizing, color, size, graphs**
    *   **Making a graph, so that you can see the changes in visualization or comparison**

**"Which work method is easier?
Is Kaizen a gain or a loss for you?"**

2. **Just talking = empty responses**

3. **One Kaizen report = periodical inspection of your work.**

4. **Review the way you do your job.**

5. **Institutionalization of the Kaizen habit.**

6. **If you don't do anything, the employees will just maintain the status quo.**

7. **To enhance the workforce through Kaizen:**

    - **Discuss specific Kaizen examples**
    - **Use your own workplace examples**
    - **No more unnecessary discussion**
    - **No more unnecessary misunderstanding**

8. **Kaizen for workforce improvement**

Everyday focus	Short-term effect	Long-term result
Kaizen	Series of small resistance	Growing by solving problems sequentially
Normal daily work	Very little resistance	No growth at all

The Idea Generator – Quick and Easy Kaizen

9.   Kaizen should be done to benefit you, the employee.

10. With Kaizen you can change yourself and you can
      change your workplace.

Quick & Easy KAIZEN	
Before Improvement	*After Improvement*
The effect:	
Date:	**Name:**

Quick & Easy KAIZEN	
Before Improvement	*After Improvement*
The effect:	
Date:	**Name:**

Chapter 9: The Power of Accumulating Small Change

> *"Continuous process improvement helps us understand what we are doing right and what we are doing wrong and what we can do to improve."*
> **Bryan Bergsteinsson, VP Lexus**

By Developing and Accumulating Your Own Examples, You Can Change Knowledge into Wisdom

So far, we've talked about Kaizen-type principles such as Kaizen by visualization and Kaizen by changing the method so that you don't have to say, "be careful." Also, we talked about how, even though it's not perfect, if any Kaizen can improve something a little bit it is a good Kaizen. At this time, stop and think about your own work environment and see if you can think about situations where these principles can be applied.

As you think about your workplace, write down your ideas on blank Kaizen forms. Use the following lists to help you discover opportunities for improvement.

Possible Problem areas to be considered might include:

Customer service – can be improved
Quality - can be improved

Costs - can be lowered
Schedule - improve delivery and production time
Cycle time, set up time - can be reduced
Inventory - reduce the unnecessary stock
Safety - reduce possible accidents
People - improve worker's skills and knowledge
Equipment - improve downtime and efficiency
Environment - improve air quality, reduce odors
Visual - use colors, clean up, find things easier
Location or distance - reduce unnecessary motion or
      facilitate necessary interaction, etc.

You might want to reduce noise, increase lighting, or do other things that will improve the efficiency of the work place and improve the quality of the work life.

Possible ways for changing might involve:

Changing your viewpoint or your position
Changing your steps or methods
Changing the way you are combining things
Changing materials and parts
Changing in a "pinch" or in a difficult time
Changing negative to positive
Changing the timing, etc.

The Kaizen Opportunity Matrix

You can then develop a matrix to begin looking for opportunities using the Kaizen principles in areas under your control to suggest possible small items for improvement.

Exhibit 9-1 One example of Kaizen Opportunity Matrix

Problem	Searching for small change targets to attack			
	Positions	Methods	Parts	Angles
Quality				X
Costs			X	
Schedule		X		
Safety		X		

Write down Kaizen ideas

Next, you can write down your own Kaizen ideas or other people's:

- **Write down ideas you had in the past and solved.**
- **Write down a change that you would like to make, a small change, state the problem, the solution and the effect.**
- **Write down problems you have now that need solutions.**
- **Remember we are looking for small changes.**

By writing down your ideas, you can internalize these principles of Kaizen and make them your own. By writing down your ideas, you are actually changing the knowledge you gained from reading this book into your own wisdom. By just reading a book, all you end up doing is increasing knowledge. By applying, by making a connection with what you learn to your own job, then you can make its wisdom useful in your workplace. In other words, you are developing your ability to adapt or apply knowledge to your own workplace.

The examples used in this book are there to stimulate your own ideas. By adding your own Kaizen examples, then you can make this training material your own. In Kaizen activity, like in an implementation activity, the ultimate goal is to develop your own Kaizen material. There are many Kaizen examples. Therefore, if you can group them and make it usable for other people, then you can develop an excellent Kaizen textbook for your own workplace.

Sharing knowledge by using a compilation of examples.

At the beginning, simply sorting out your Kaizen examples by types or principles would be sufficient. By putting the examples into order, you will be developing your own company's Kaizen training manual. Maybe you can even find your own unique principles of Kaizen, or you can say that you are accumulating your own company's Kaizen know-how.

The Idea Generator – Quick and Easy Kaizen

Quick & Easy KAIZEN	
Before Improvement	**After Improvement**

The effect:

Date: **Name:**

Three Principles of Kaizen Implementation

*"Creativity is allowing yourself
to make mistakes. Art is knowing
which ones to keep."*
Scott Adams

There are two problems in Quick and Easy Kaizen activities. One issue is with implementing Kaizen and the other is in visualizing or surfacing those Kaizens. The first issue of implementing Quick and Easy Kaizen can be easily solved when you understand the following three basic approaches to Kaizen. (Remember, you don't have to be perfect to do Kaizen.) You can:

3 Principles to Implementing Kaizen

- **Attack by changing a part, not the whole.**
- **Attack by changing the angle.**
- **Attack by changing the level.**

First, if you want to change the whole thing, it is very difficult. It often requires large-scale countermeasures. You cannot implement and materialize your idea for a long time. This is a poor approach for Kaizen. Those people, who are good at Kaizen, do not attempt to solve the whole problem at once. They focus on what they can do. Since they focus on what they can do, they can implement their ideas quickly. The difference is just like that, that's all it is. **Focus on what you can do.**

In general, dividing something into parts makes it easier to understand. Likewise, if you divide something into parts, it is easier to do it. This is what we mean by starting with parts. Start by dividing things into smaller parts, and attack little by little and change little by little. This is a major principle of Kaizen.

Secondly, we don't stick to only one way of doing things. Look at things from different angles and then try to change the factors involving that situation or change the conditions. If this one doesn't work, try that one. If that one doesn't work, let's do this or something like that. If vertical doesn't work, try horizontal or if horizontal doesn't work maybe make it diagonal. In other words, look at different angles; it's the knack of selecting means, selecting methods. This is a key to Quick and Easy Kaizen implementation.

Thirdly, it is not necessary to be perfect in Kaizen. As we have said, the best is the enemy of Kaizen. People who want to be perfect from the beginning are not good at Kaizen. They are too tensed up and cannot do much. However, those who are good at Kaizen clearly understand that the goal of Kaizen is to make something just a little bit better, a *minor* improvement. If the countermeasure seems to be too formidable, they will lower the level to start what they can do to the extent that they can do it.

Problem:
A meter is placed high up on a wall. To read the meter you have to climb a ladder. It could be dangerous to climb the ladder to check the meter.

Solution:
#1   You can tie a lifeline around your waste so that if you slip off the ladder the lifeline would hold you back.

#2   You could make it easier to climb by wearing special gloves and shoes with anti-skid material.

#3   You could connect a simple mirror or video camera to display the meter without having to climb the ladder.

This is finding solutions by looking at different angles or levels, from best to better to better.

Tentatively at first!

"At once, large scale and fundamental changes."

Start where you can begin.

"Too big, I can't do it."

Change

Start by changing a part, not a whole.

Quick & Easy KAIZEN	
Before Improvement	**After Improvement**

The effect:

Date: **Name:**

The Smaller Kaizen is a Better Kaizen

"And gain is gain, however small. "
Robert Browning

A trivial Kaizen is a good Kaizen: Kaizen means changing, from right to left, from vertical to horizontal etc.

When looking at the simple Kaizen examples, people tend to say, "They only changed from right to left. You just changed from upward to downward. That's all." People sometimes, unfortunately, look down at these simple Kaizen examples.

This is a typical misunderstanding of Kaizen. If you change from vertical to horizontal, and you can gain a little bit of effect, then that is an excellent Kaizen. If you can change from right to left and still get a good effect, then that is wonderful. To those people who look down on simple examples, I would like to offer the phrase "Trivial Kaizen is good Kaizen."

Kaizen means continuous change. It could be from vertical to horizontal, from right to left, changing positions, changing angles, changing levels, and changing parts; it is an endless dynamic process.

We should always try to remember what our purpose is in doing Kaizen. **We want to motivate people to be self-actualized, to participate fully, and have a sense of ownership and pride in themselves and the work that they do.** We want to give people the opportunity to be creative and to be part of our continuous im-

187

provement activities. We want people to be excited about and look forward to coming to work every day. Through Kaizen activities we can challenge people to improve by making little improvements within their own work area. So even very small Kaizens are very good if they inspire people to feel a real sense of accomplishment and ownership in their work.

Please notice that we're not saying, "even a trivial Kaizen is good." We're not using "even." **We're saying the more trivial, the better. We want it to be easy to do. We want people to be involved in the change process. Of course, we want great ideas and we totally accept them but, as we have said earlier, we do not want the great ideas to stop the continuous flow of small changes that are meaningful to every worker.**

> *"Don't ignore the small things –*
> *the kite flies because of its tail."*
> **American Proverb**

Trivial Kaizens, very small changes, are valuable. A trivial Kaizen, a small Kaizen, means that you can do it simply and quickly. It is a positive reflection of the person who can come up with new improvement ideas. It means that she has the ability really to trace something down to the root cause. If that person has the ability to trace down, dig down to the root cause, then she can identify the small causes of the problem, and then fix the problem or cause. And the counter-measure can also be very small.

Question:
What is Kaizen?

Answer:
To draw just one line is Kaizen.

188

As an example, in a typical factory on machines there are many nuts and bolts. It is very difficult to tell just by looking at a bolt if one is loose. Periodically maintenance people would take many hours to tighten all of the nuts and bolts to insure against any potential problems that could be caused by a loose bolt. They would try to tighten all of the bolts with a wrench even those that were not loose. But, if one white or black line was drawn across the bolt when it was tight then just by a visual glance you could tell if there had been any slippage. Just one line on the bolt saves countless hours.

Maintenance people would have to tighten all of the nuts and bolts even those that were not loose because at a glance you could not tell which ones were loose.

But now with just one line painted across the bolt you can tell at a glance when the bolt has moved.

Only one line is Kaizen and it does save an enormous amount of time.

Another example:

At the office filing folders improperly is very easy to do. And then when you look for a specific folder, you can't find it because it has been misfiled. But just drawing one line across the folders tells the mind at a glance when one is out of place.

 Searching, looking for a misplaced file folder.

Draw just one line across the files when they are in proper order.

 At a glance you can tell when a file folder is filed out of order.

Just one line is a Kaizen.

"What you just changed right to left! You just moved something. It is so ordinary. It shouldn't be called a kaizen!"

"If it gained results it is wonderful."

Trivial kaizen is good. The more trivial the better.

Acupuncture is an alternative medical system based on the idea that little tiny needles placed at the right place in your body can cause a shift to well being. Chiropractors also believe that the slight manipulation of your bones and muscles can bring new health. Homeopathy, another alternative system, believes that the smaller the dosage of a remedy, the greater the effect. All of these methods support the idea that all the body needs is a very tiny "push," to change direction. It is another of those laws of physics. "A body at rest tends to stay at rest." It is called inertia. We just resist change. Why, we can't be sure. But there is another law of physics that applies here, "A body in motion tends to stay in motion." Like with acupuncture or homeopathy, a very small shift can get us started in a new direction. And then one small change after another can keep us moving in that new direction.

We know the enormous power within the atom. The atom is minuscule in size but extremely potent. The atom is potentially explosive, and when a chain reaction takes place enormous energy is released. Size in and of itself does not solve our problems. That is why we want you to always consider the small things as potentially powerful, for it allows everyone in the workplace to make improvements.

Those people who are good at Kaizen can identify or dig into a very small cause that is creating the problem, and then say, "It doesn't have to be that big to solve this problem. The true cause of the problem is this. We can just change a little bit on this part." By doing that they can actually implement Kaizen very quickly and simply.

Kaizen means not to expend too much labor or cost.

The background or supporting principles of a smaller Kaizen being a good Kaizen can be explained by the formula used in value engineering.

Value = Function / Cost

Function = Effect of Kaizen
Cost = The sum of money, time, labor and all other inputs

If we increase the function and either keep the cost the same or reduce the cost, the result is an increase in the value for our customers. Of course, we want to have a great effect, the bigger the effect is, the better. But the effect we are expecting from Kaizen is not that big. Kaizen is about small changes. Therefore, a small effect is fine for Kaizen; even small effects increase the value of our products and services.

The Idea Generator – Quick and Easy Kaizen

In Part IV there are interviews with Dana Corporation executives and managers. For the past 10 years, Dana's 75,000 employees have submitted over 2,000,000 ideas each year with an 80% implementation rate. They still get the big ideas, the new products, the new equipment, the new processes, but they also have virtually everyone involved and excited about their jobs.

Anthony Miriello, my 16-year-old grandson, was given an interesting homework assignment by his high school science teacher—an experiment. Anthony was asked to buy a small mousetrap and then to build a "mousetrap car" using the energy released from the mousetrap to move the car forward. The instructions from the teacher were very simple. Everything else was up to the student's imagination. Well, Anthony spent hours upon hours finding new ways to build his car, first with very small wheels made from bottle tops, then with CD ROM disks to give the car more power. The CDs were the two front wheels with a small pole used as the axle and the tops of colored markers to hold the axle to the wheels. He then found an old piece of plastic to use as the body of the car and a medicine bottle top for the single rear wheel. It was a three-wheeled car. He wrapped a string around the axle and tied it to the mousetrap, which moved the car forward when released.

When I saw Anthony, he was already working on his third version of the car, and it moved around 4 meters when the mousetrap was snapped. However, just a few days later when he turned the project over to his teacher, his car traveled 12 meters.

Anthony excitedly worked and reworked on his project. He loved the challenge. It was a very creative exercise, which is always an ideal way to learn. In fact, I believe that creativity is the only means by which people can truly be involved in any organization.

Kaizen works the same way. Give people the challenge to change. Give them some hints but let them be creative on their own and you will find a new excitement in the workplace. Give them just a small challenge.

Cost is, of course, an important thing to any company. How much time do you spend, how much labor does it cost and how much money do you expend on this Kaizen? The value of Kaizen is in coming up with an idea so that you don't have to spend much money, but yet you are still improving the situation even a little bit. Each little idea has a small effect but, added together, they represent great power to the company, and they do generate real excitement for the worker.

People who are good at Kaizen are good at coming up with the ways or the ideas or the method that doesn't require much money. Small Kaizens do not require much money. As people often say, "If you don't have money, use your brain."

What's more, if the effect is the same, the more valuable Kaizens are the ones that do not require time, labor, or cost. That's why simple Kaizen is better.

It is very hard to make big changes, for you often find all kinds of resistance from those around you.

Start small. Begin by chipping away with small changes and you can eventually get rid of the problem.

Since we don't have enough money, we change from horizontal to vertical. Since we don't have enough space, we do it horizontally. Since we don't have enough time, we do it vertically.

Here is a great example of a simple change from horizontal to vertical. In some areas traffic lights have red, yellow and green lights arranged horizontally, rather than vertically, with a special cover that helps the driver to see it more easily. However, in snowy areas, the snow piles up over these covers every winter. Over time the metal weakens from the weight of the snow and can eventually break. Therefore, in snowy areas these traffic lights need to be made stronger than in other areas. Of course, if you have a large budget you can build those very heavy metal traffic lights. However, budgets were limited, and requests were many.

A government office that doesn't have Kaizen principles in mind might have said "We don't have the budget so we cannot meet your request; you'll have to wait." However, these people looked at the root of the problem, they thought about small things they could do instead of large-scale exorbitant changes. Their solution? Change the existing traffic lights from horizontal to vertical. By doing that, much less snow can accumulate over the cover and it doesn't require such hard material. Therefore, they didn't need to spend as much. This is an example of a simple, and effective change from horizontal to vertical. Even with that kind of small change, you can expect a big effect. That is a wonderful Kaizen.

Horizontal traffic signal.

The Idea Generator – Quick and Easy Kaizen

Vertical traffic signal.

Horizontal slot or vertical slot

A familiar example would be the coin slots in vending machines. There are two types, the vertical slot and horizontal slot. The vending machine for soft drinks usually is horizontal. On the other hand, the ticket machine slots at railway stations are vertical. That is not just based on their slot-making preferences; there are good reasons for this.

After a coin is dropped into the vertical coin slot for a ticketing machine, it drops, then rolls. In the horizontal arrangement, the coin slides instead, which takes more time, but allows the machine to be thinner. These days, especially, most vending machines have to be thinner so that they won't occupy too much space. Moreover, the horizontal arrangement allows more space inside the machine, so soft drink companies, for example, can fit more cans inside the machine.

On the other hand, the train station ticket machine has a vertical coin slot. Tickets are small and don't take up much space inside the machine. What's more, the ticketing machine is usually

197

stored inside the station building where there is plenty of room for it. Therefore, space is not the issue, but speed is. People who are trying to catch a train have limited time. They want to buy it quickly. Therefore the slot is vertical.

It's simple. By making the coin slot vertical, you can gain speed. With a horizontal slot, you gain space.

However, changing from vertical to horizontal is not always that simple, but it can be very effective. Here is an even more fa-mous example to explain this effect.

There was a person who did not make money on one of his most important inventions because he did not change from vertical to horizontal. His name was Thomas Edison. Thomas Edison was very famous for his many inventions, including the electric light bulb and the phonograph. The phonograph, however, did not make Thomas Edison much money. The people who made money from this invention were those who changed it from vertical to horizon-tal.

Thomas Edison's phonograph had a cylinder shape and the recording went on the vertical cylinder. But this shape was not suitable for large-scale manufacturing. Soon other manufacturers changed from vertical to horizontal, and it became a circular record. By making this one change, it became possible to produce them in large quantities and records became very popular throughout the world. And those people who made the disc-type records made a fortune.

Of course, the phonograph is a very big invention, which will probably always be considered an important part of human history. Ordinary people do not make this kind of monumental invention.

The Idea Generator – Quick and Easy Kaizen

However, changing something that already exists from horizontal to vertical is possible for us ordinary people. It doesn't require that much ingenuity or talent. Therefore, even we can challenge genius with small changes.

Cylinder-type phonograph

Disc-type phonograph.
Shown as Emile Berliner's first disc record player

Someday We Might Be Driving a Lexus, a Mercedes Benz, or a Rolls Royce, but We Begin with a Bicycle

"I think self-awareness is probably the most important thing towards being a champion."
Billie Jean King

Now here is an example of changing from a vertical to a horizontal arrangement in the workplace. In one company they were producing a rectangular shaped product, and since it was a large product, the workers had to climb a ladder or steps to work on the top and do their job. Of course, if you go up there is always a risk of falling down. You also need to bring all your tools up to the top with you to work, and to do that you must be careful not to drop anything.

If this were not a Kaizen company, supervisors would just say, "Be careful." Some employees may complain that it is cumbersome to go up and down all the time, and the veteran employees would say, "We've always done it that way, don't complain, just do it as we always have." Well, one day a man in that company said, "How about laying this product down sideways? Then we don't have to climb up and down and we don't have to worry about falling." Of course, once somebody says it, it is obvious. In this situation, there was no problem changing from a vertical to a horizontal arrangement, so they decided to lay the product down.

By doing that they can work on the product easily, safely and speedily. This is a very good example of improving the situation by just changing from vertical to horizontal. Given the same problem, those people who are not good at Kaizen tend to think only in terms of "big things." How about we install a mechanism to raise the floor up and down so that we don't have to climb up and down the ladder? Of course, if you have an elevated mechanism installed in the floor to make it go up and down, that would be the best. But, that cannot be done immediately. Maybe you could do it when the old factory is remodeled or a new plant is built. However, you cannot do it immediately. It would probably take a few years or so. So how are you going handle the situation in the meanwhile? Well, you can just complain and continue to do the job as it has been done, climbing up and down. Or you can lay the product down horizontally.

Exhibit 9-2 Kaizen with vertical and horizontal change

Before Improvement	After Improvement
To assemble work on this box-type product you needed to climb up steps.	It has been changed and laid-down horizontally.

The Effect   Since we do not need to use steps, the work became safer and easier because we did not have to bring parts and materials up with us.

As we have stated, in most cases large-scale improvements cannot be done immediately. However, small and trivial things can be done immediately. So you can get an improvement effect without delay. That is the strength of Kaizen.

Quick & Easy KAIZEN	
Before Improvement	**After Improvement**
The effect:	
Date:	**Name:**

Summary:

1. **Kaizen is quick and easy to**

- **Implement**
- **Write down**

2. **Basic principles for Kaizen implementation**

The Idea Generator – Quick and Easy Kaizen

- **Start with a part**
- **Look at multiple angles**
- **Look at multiple levels**

3. Focus on what you can do. Do not attempt to solve the whole problem once.

4. Kaizen means continuous small change: vertical to horizontal, right to left, changing positions, changing angles, changing levels; it is an endless dynamic process.

5. We want people to have a sense of ownership and pride in themselves and the work that they do.

6. The valuable Kaizen is a small Kaizen.

7. Value = Function / Cost. Even small changes add value.

Part III

The Supporting Environment: How to Establish and Maintain a Corporate Culture for Quick and Easy Kaizen System

Sharing Kaizen with Others Leads to Continuous Kaizen and Kaizen Taking Root in the Work Place, Stabilizing, Then Becoming Your Own

Part III Overview

Here we look at the process of installing a Quick and Easy Kaizen system and sustaining it.

Dr. Shigeo Shingo, the genius behind the Toyota Production System known as JIT or Lean production, after every consulting assignment or training session would end with the words, "Do it!" He was well ahead of Nike with that phrase. "Do it. Don't postpone it. Don't find an excuse not to do it. Do it. Do it now."

Everyone has the creative potential and the fundamental right to participate and express themselves in making decisions that affect them and in improving the products and services. Stop and look freshly at the people working with you and begin to ask them for their ideas. You will be amazed – like opening a Pandora's box. Some of the ideas you might not like, some of the ideas maybe threatening to you personally. Just listen. Let it all come out. Take it all as just information to deal with. And then watch the "magic" take place. You can transform the workplace, your environment will change, and your employees and your customers will be happier.

In this Part III we hope to tie it all together and answer most of your questions about implementing Quick and Easy Kaizen and sustaining it.

Chapter 10: The Kaizen Process

"Excellence is the gradual result
of always striving to do better."
Pat Riley

The beginning

You started the process by reading this book on your own. Next, you might like to begin discussing what you have read with your associates in the company. See if it in anyway excites them with the possibility of getting the workers really involved, really participating in the improvement of their very own jobs, their very own work environment, and starting to feel a real sense of ownership. What greater feeling is there than to come up with an idea, install it yourself, and share it with your supervisors and your peer group? "Yes, I did a very simple Kaizen that reduced wastage on the job."

Every job has its problems. But most often we just live with the problems. Now with Kaizen there is an opportunity to create a whole new mindset to attack those little but annoying problems that are significant to every worker individually, and can collectively save time and money for the company.

Jack Simms, at Dana Corporation, told me a nice little story about a woman in his company who was disposing of a great deal of waste paper on her job. She would open the mail and then periodically, during the day, she would get up and walk across the room to dump the waste paper into a basket. When taught Kaizen, she came up with the small idea to move the basket next to her desk. Now, this is very simple and you might say, "Well that is obvious, it should have been done earlier." But, it wasn't done until she came up with the idea and wrote it down as her Kaizen. She now saves a little time during each workday.

Jack also mentioned another woman who was printing out around 900 pages a day on her computer. The problem was that for some reason every time the printer printed a page it also printed two blank pages. She just thought it was a computer problem that she had to live with.

Well, that office worker initially thought that the problem would have to be solved by some software engineer. While thinking about Kaizen with her new 'Kaizen Mindset,' she herself came up with the solution and solved the problem.

Do Kaizen yourself

Try writing down every problem that occurs during the day, no matter how small. "My pen doesn't work," "the printer wastes paper," "I forget to take my pills." Jack Simms, once again, solved his pill problem by taking a picture of his pill and pillbox and putting them on his screen saver so that every time now when he looks at his computer he sees the pills as a reminder to take them. It is simple, but very effective.

As you do Kaizen yourself, as often as you can, you start to experience the constant generation of ideas and you start to acquire real power from doing it. You can teach others from your own experience.

The Idea Generator – Quick and Easy Kaizen

Not long ago, I noticed that I have too much paper in my baskets on my desk. Anything that interests me but does not relate to what I am doing at the moment gets dumped into this "I-will-get-around-to-it pile," or goes into the "to-be-filed box." Problem is that the baskets get higher and higher. I will change my procedure. From now on I will tag every item with a "read date or disposal date." I will make sure the basket is kept in date order. And then I will make a commitment to either read it on that date or dispose of it. So if you will excuse me for the moment, I will attack the paper basket. Don't go away I will be back real soon...

See, it didn't take that long to do! A very simple Kaizen, but it should help me be a little bit more productive.

The bulletin board

After the Kaizen is implemented and written down, then one way of sharing it with others is to post it and all other Kaizens on the bulletin board where everyone can see them. It is a simple way to get recognition. And it would be good to have a daily or weekly review session whereby everyone in the department gathers around the bulletin board and each person reads one of their Kaizens for a brief question and answer session.

We also advise gathering people for a daily 10-minute Kaizen session to ask them what problems occurred during the day and if anyone has any ideas on how to solve those problems. Especially when you want to serve customers, it is very powerful to ask people daily about any problems that might have occurred over the telephone or in the store. Information sharing sessions can really help make substantial improvements.

The Promoter

Often it is easy to get excited about something new and do it—for a while. But, after a short period of time, many of us go back to the "same old way." We fall back into the old routine. Like the adage, "Water tends to flow in the same direction," unless you build a dam or dig a new ditch. Well, Kaizen is about changing the method so that we can't go back to the same old ways. We don't want Kaizen to just be another, "flavor of the month," where we get a great new management idea and then it wanes and disappears.

So, we need a promoter. We need someone who becomes responsible to encourage, to stimulate, and to challenge others to continuously write down and share their Kaizens. In some plants it is the plant manager, in some other plants or in offices it is a person whose single most important job is to teach, support, and promote the Kaizen system.

The reward system

At Dana Corporation, every plant or office has a different method, but normally no direct cash award is given for ideas submitted. Some plants might share profits or have special drawings. However, in Japan, many companies offer 500 yen for an implemented idea (that's a little less than US $5), 1,000 yen for a more highly creative idea, and a possible 10,000 yen (close to US $100) for the best ideas of the month.

Some people claim the financial reward is not necessary as Kaizen is considered part of their jobs. In one of our interviews in

The Idea Generator – Quick and Easy Kaizen

Part IV of the book, a Dana manager mentions that there are no financial rewards; none are needed. They are getting an average of 36 ideas per year per employee. In some environments money might be the necessary stimulant, and at other places it might not be necessary. If it stimulates people to get a little bit more excited about doing Kaizen, then test various methods to see what works for you. Do good accounting and measure the overall effects of Kaizen in profit, in employee morale, in turnover, in reduction of waste, in attracting new employees, in customer satisfaction, etc.

At Toyota plants in the US, the rewards systems are slightly different. At the Georgetown, Kentucky plant, for each implemented Kaizen a worker will receive a reward, with a minimum of a $20.00 gift certificate. If they accumulate $500.00 or more, they can turn the certificates into cash. And if the idea saves the company money, the worker can share in that savings up to $25,000. They received around 18 ideas per worker in the year 2000.

At TABC, another Toyota plant in California, the rewards start at $5.00 and can go up to $1,000, but they are receiving only 6 or 7 ideas per worker year.

At NUMMI, a joint venture between General Motors and Toyota, the minimum is $6.00. Even a rejected idea is given $3.00, and the reward can reach up to $15,000.

The systems at Toyota meld the Japanese and the American suggestion systems. One major problem is that not everyone participates. At one Toyota plant, with a goal of 80% participation, only 57% of the employees submitted improvement ideas. Also, since many of the ideas are for other people to implement, and also the ideas must be evaluated for monetary rewards, it takes considerable time for the worker to get feedback on their submitted ideas.

211

There could be a gap of a month or several months before a worker hears if the idea is accepted. This might be a reason for the lower participation rate. But still, the system at Toyota is far better than at most other American companies—at least employees are surfacing new ideas.

Probably a better system would be to use Quick and Easy Kaizen for the stream of small ideas, and also have another system for suggestions and ideas that need time to evaluate.

At Dana, a worker normally knows within 24 hours if their idea has been accepted. In most plants that have Quick and Easy Kaizen in Japan, the worker either immediately implements the idea or is given immediate feedback from their supervisor. We feel the immediate feedback system is ideal. Quick and Easy Kaizen is a motivational system to help keep people interested, excited about their jobs, and the faster the response time from their supervisors the better.

The target

Woody Morcott, the previous chairman of Dana Corporation, came back from a trip to Japan and challenged everyone in the company to come up with two improvement ideas per month.

As a result, the managers were all forced to shift their attitudes about their employees' new ideas. In the past, an employee would approach his manager with an idea only to have the manager find "holes" in the idea and tell him why the idea wasn't good.

We will let you in on a little secret: **"You can always find holes in another person's idea, always."**

212

The Idea Generator – Quick and Easy Kaizen

Some people have a better talent in finding those "holes" than others. Recognize this truism and, instead of finding a hole, look for a way to encourage and help the employee improve or come up with another Kaizen to improve the original Kaizen. You **do this by challenging the employee, not by telling him.**

At first, an idea might seem just too simple, or it might even sound like wrong thinking. But instead of rejecting the idea outright, you should encourage the worker to look at the problem from another point of view. Give her another chance to think through the problem and come up with another variable.

When an employee comes up with an idea, the supervisor in the past often thought that it was his job to come up with ideas and the worker should "just do his job," or the supervisor might have felt that the new idea was some kind of threat to his position.

We are now in a new age. We need everyone in the company to be creative.

Criticism

Be very careful with criticism. If you criticize an idea, you might close the employee forever. You should consider every idea as an honest attempt by the employees to express themselves. The initial idea might not seem valid to you, but with some care on your part, you might be able to explore further with the employee to modify the idea, to redirect it slightly so as to allow the creative process to continue. You never know when a really bad idea might lead to a very good one! I have quoted Marie Curie several times in this book. She and her husband went through hundreds if not thousands of failures before they discovered powerful and beneficial uses for radioactivity.

Rejected ideas

Be careful! When a person submits an unworkable idea, you want to show support and gratitude and carefully explain why the idea might not work at this time. But do offer suggestions for improvement. Ask them to rethink the problem and try to find other solutions. Do not criticize the person, only carefully review the problem. You do need tact, for you do not want to curb the employee's enthusiasm to submit future Kaizens.

One good way to handle an unworkable idea is to ask the employee's work team to discuss the idea. People seem to more open and readably accept reviews from their peer group then from their supervisors. The teams should be taught how to carefully discuss the ideas to discover the intention of the idea presenter, and seek ways to alter or shift thinking about how to solve the problem. The person submitting the idea is showing that they do want to participate in the idea process. The employee recognizes a problem and you want to develop a mechanism that will help them find a solution.

Recognition

Recognition can come from the financial rewards, but the old "pat on the back," or "thank you for a job well done," is most appropriate. Use your company newsletter, or stop everyone for a few moments to express your excitement and appreciation.

The Idea Generator – Quick and Easy Kaizen

When I managed a data processing company in the Caribbean, I would often stop everyone, maybe 75 people at a time, and share some information that I thought was important to them. I really loved those breaks.

Daily reminders

The Nordstrom department store manager gets on the speaker system for 10 minutes every single day and reminds people about their single most important issue, "pleasing customers."

At a football or basketball game the crowd is the reminder. There, the audience "shouts and screams," their approval. Well, it isn't a bad idea to ring the bell every time someone brings up his or her completed Kaizen.

We all come up with ideas—we are making a system out of it, and you will see it explode. Instead of it being done haphazardly, it is now a management improvement process. It is powerful and it works.

Convincing management

Either ask your supervisor to read this book or take selected pictures and charts, then make a presentation. We like to teach a three-hour introductory course on Quick and Easy Kaizen, with the goal that before the end of the course the participants are writing out their Kaizens in three minutes, in less than 75 words.

Leadership

Quick and Easy Kaizen works and works well, but it must be supported by management. **It is a great communication tool, keeping management informed about people's improvement ideas and the problems faced on the job.** To work well, Quick and Easy Kaizen needs dedicated management that is willing to recognize that each person has hidden talents yet to be revealed. It needs commitment to the pursuit of excellence; recognizing that excellence can only happen when every employee is given the opportunity to fully participate in the improvement process. The great leaders know how to inspire people to reach beyond their limitations to succeed. All it requires is for the leader to stay focused and make Quick and Easy Kaizen part of their daily responsibility. Read Pat Pilleri's interview and the other Dana interviews at the back of the book. Pat Pilleri manages a plant with 750 people and yet he is able to spend 50% of his workday listening to employees. He reads every idea submitted by workers and delegates these ideas to his staff members who are instructed to respond to the person who submitted the idea within 24 hours. It is amazing what happens when people know that there is someone who listens and respects their ideas.

Running the first training session

You are reading the book and now it is time to make the material come "alive" for you. Use the material in the book and run your training session, or invite us to come in and run the first session with you.

As we've said, doing Kaizen without a follow-up is to be avoided. Reading this book is the same way. We hope you are enjoying the book, but now it is your challenge to excite others around you to start writing their ideas down quickly and easily.

We recommend that you either put together your in-house seminar to teach the principles in this book or call us to run a three-hour seminar to get you started. Sometimes you need an external force. There is the saying, "A prophet is never known unto his own house." So, if you like, bring us in and we will get you started and then you can carry on.

The book's real value comes when you quickly and easily start your own in-house Kaizen program. You want people to implement their ideas, write them down, and share them with others. Not just once, but continuously. Then you can expect some results. Persistence is the key to implementing and practicing what you have learned from this book.

By writing Kaizens again and again, within three minutes each, people really feel it is possible.

Feeling the Knowledge and Implementing

Just understanding what is written in this book and keeping it in your head doesn't make it a reality in your workplace. You are taking valuable time to read this book, and now is the time to put the knowledge into action. But it is not the knowledge that moves people. It is your energy in teaching and getting them to write down their Kaizens.

Today we can take in the scenery of the world from the comfort of home through many different television channels, the Internet, and so forth. So does that mean you don't need to travel anymore? That's not true. The more information you get on exotic places in the world, the more people seem to want to go on trips so that they can experience the places for themselves: to hear exotic animals in the rainforest, smell fresh herbs in the fields of Provence, taste Limoncello in Umbria, feel the spray of the rugged Tasman Sea. It is time to leave the comfort of your reading chair and experience Kaizen for yourself.

There was a big debate in the past among sporting groups if games should be shown on TV for free. The people who opposed this said, "If we broadcast it live, that will be sufficient and nobody will come to see it." But when the broadcasting started, the number of people coming to the live game actually increased. Those people who were interested in the sport came to see the action so that they could feel a part of the experience as well. You, too, might find reading this book and doing Kaizen to be two entirely different things.

Super fast, impressive method

Should the teacher in the seminar use a loud voice and lots of animation? It depends. The great master from his depth of experience and past reputation can speak more calmly and slowly, and still capture the entire audience who waits to hear the words of wisdom. Mr. Taiichi Ohno, the co-inventor of the Toyota Production System, lectured like that. When the Japan Human Resource Association invited him to lecture at their Kaizen office, he was at the later stages of his life, and his health was poor. He spoke very softly and not so smoothly, but he was very calm. Yet more than 1,000 people in the audience were drawn to his talk; they were captivated by his lecture. That is the kind of thing that only a few, really accomplished and special people in this world could do.

Some day, with luck, we might each receive that extraordinary level of respect and appreciation from others. But for now we have to shout, dance, and do whatever is necessary to keep our audience excited and awake. Miraculously, it works for both of the authors of this book.

Quick & Easy KAIZEN	
Before Improvement	**After Improvement**
The effect:	
Date:	**Name:**

Creating a Kaizen Culture

Implementation of Kaizen is Easy. The Remaining Problem is How to Promote and Surface Kaizen More Effectively.

*"I can't understand why people
are frightened of new ideas. I'm
frightened of the old ones."*

John Cage

Although we talked about the three principles of Kaizen implementation—you attack part of a problem, not the whole problem; you change the angle and you change the level—those are probably things that everybody has been doing unconsciously. Once they recognize this, they are sure to think it is obvious, even ordinary.

Already, we each adapt to difficult situations or conditions that we are in and "do what we can do." That is fine. We want to do what we can do, but to make a change we must start with a part. We start making change in small increments.

Of course, when you teach Kaizen, you don't have to use the words "three principles." we can do Kaizen without really understanding the three basic principles. But if you understand these three principles and use them consciously, it can help to promote Kaizen activities more effectively.

For example, maybe a subordinate reports to you and says to you one day, "I cannot do Kaizen very well." Then you might discuss how this person is approaching Kaizen. There is a good chance that the problem is he's trying to change the whole thing at once. You can tell him to focus on what he can do. Or you might ask, "Are you trying to stick to only one method? That might inhibit Kaizen. Look at the situation from different angles and try many different methods."

Exhibit 10-1 Small Kaizen made by changing the angle

Before improvement:	After improvement:
Fire hose was run over by a forklift, now not usable	Instead of discarding the entire hose, we got the Fire Department to fix it for us
Effect: Fire hose now available and repaired at no cost	
Submitted By: E. Team	

You could also ask, "Are you trying to be perfect from the beginning?" Explain that Kaizen works even when there is very little improvement. That is fine. Advise the worker, "Begin with something minor you can do right now."

Remind your employees that Quick and Easy Kaizen should not be difficult. We are not encouraging people to make big changes; we are saying you don't have to do what you cannot do. All you need to do is what you can do. That is Kaizen. Therefore, Kaizen implementation is not difficult.

We want to create a Kaizen culture.

So the only remaining hurdle in making Kaizen activity a successful addition to your workplace is writing it down. Kaizen does not stop after the installation of the idea; **it must be documented, it must be surfaced for others to see in the workplace.** Companies that neglect this important part of Kaizen are not making big progress. We encourage you to take this opportunity right now to write another Kaizen in memo form. Use any ideas you have jotted down so far, and remember 3 minutes and 75 words or less. Go!

Quick & Easy KAIZEN	
Before Improvement	*After Improvement*
The effect:	
Date:	Name:

From Unconscious Kaizen to Conscious Kaizen

"We must change in order to survive."
Pearl Bailey

Kaizen is a simple thing, and everybody to a certain extent is already doing it unconsciously in his or her daily work. For example, concise reporting is a basic function of most jobs, especially when you make a change. It is essential that you inform the others around you of the change, and informing them in writing is a great way to do that—especially when the writing is brief and to the point, as in a memo. When we record ideas for Kaizen, it should also be concise and simple, like jotting down a memo. It should be within 75 words and completed in three minutes.

That's Kaizen!

We now understand that a Kaizen report should be done very simply. Those people who are in a position to coach and promote Kaizen need to say, "That's Kaizen!" frequently as positive reinforcement. There are many ways to say it, too. Find your own voice and practice saying, "That's Kaizen!" in your own way.

This kind of reinforcement is especially important so that the people who did the Kaizen are aware that they did Kaizen. Otherwise they might think that their simple Kaizens are not worthy of being written down and shared with others. Now is the time to support and praise people and tell them how great their ideas are and how much you appreciate their efforts. "That's too little. That

223

is too obvious. That's common sense. Why do it now?" These are all statements to avoid.

Many people are already doing Kaizen, yet they believe it is not good enough, not big enough. So even though good Kaizens are going on, **they are not surfacing** and they disappear into the darkness and then cannot be shared. You can play an important part in making sure they are brought into daylight and everyone understands that small Kaizens are important Kaizens.

> **Many people are already doing Kaizen yet they believe it is not good enough.**
>
> **They are not surfacing and sharing the results.**

If the manager simply says, "That's Kaizen! That's good!" or something like that, some people will realize they are doing more Kaizens than they were previously aware of. When they understand that one small Kaizen they've done is "good enough," they are more open to recognizing Kaizen. They say, "Well, if that was good enough, I can change a little here and change a little there," and so forth.

Little by little, they will learn to look at their jobs more consciously and see opportunities for change. That is the true aim of Kaizen. In other words, we are doing our work as we have always done it. But now we are aware of opportunities to make progress.

We want to look at our work consciously now and get motivated to change it. We want to improve the way we have

been doing it and make the work easier and more fun too. That is the ultimate goal of Kaizen.

Summary

1. Are you trying to change the whole thing?
    -   First, divide it into small increments.
    -   Start with an increment or part to the extent of what you can do.

2. Are you sticking to one method?
    -   Think from different angles.
    -   If horizontal doesn't work, try vertical.
    -   If vertical doesn't work, try diagonal.

3. Are you trying to do it perfectly from the beginning?
    -   If you can make even a little improvement, that's fine.
    -   Start with what you can do right now.

4. You don't have to do what you cannot do. Kaizen means to do what you can do.

5. You must praise and support all small improvement efforts. "That's Kaizen! That's good."

6. You are the "band leader." You bring out the best from all of your employees. You set the tempo. Everyday you encourage people to find ways to improve, to make work easier, and to have more fun!

3 Elements that make a Kaizen system work:

1. Implement – you do it
2. Surface – write it down
3. Share – post it, review it and talk about it

3 Stages of how to develop your own Kaizen system

1. Define what Kaizen is?
2. Understand why you do it, for whom do you do it for?
3. Implement and share.

Chapter 11: Utilization of Existing Functions, Systems, and Supporting Tools or Jigs

"Then the Kaizen Blitz is a period or time when we say okay, tomorrow at seven o'clock we are going to attack this portion of the facility and this is what we are going to do. We are not talking about it. We are going to do it."

Jack Simms - Dana

There are people who believe that we have to make something, create a product of some kind in order to implement Kaizen. Therefore, people tend to say that Kaizen is more suited to a factory situation, but is not so applicable to their job in sales, customer service or doing office work. Therefore, they cannot implement Kaizen. However, this is not true.

Kaizen is not just for the factory. Kaizen is an amazing tool to improve customer service for any organization. Kaizen means to select new methods to accomplish your job objectives faster and better. In other words, Kaizen means to change the way you do your job—whatever your job may be.

Of course, those workplaces that create products probably have the opportunity to change tools, the shape of the parts and so forth. Or maybe they find an opportunity to create new tools and jigs.

However, those people whose work is to communicate with somebody or, calculate, or explain things, can also use Kaizen to improve the way they do these kinds of jobs. With Kaizen, they can do these same tasks more quickly, more completely, and more effectively.

Imagine if workers just took a moment to share the problems they've encountered during the day, and solutions they may have come up with on their own, there would be incredible opportunities to improve telephone communications, internal memos, e-mails, and finding new ways to please customers.

A while back, I went into a Wolfe Camera in Portland, Oregon. I liked this particular store because they had a self-service Kodak system that allowed me to make my own enlargements. On this particular day, however, when I entered the store I looked for a clerk to help me get started. I noticed two attendants at the far end of the store and I walked over to them. However, neither one looked up at me. They were both busy hunting through packets of film. I waited for a few moments and noticed that there was no other customer in the store so I wondered why one of them couldn't just stop for a moment and serve me. Did they really want customers?

Finally one salesperson looked up right at me but didn't say a word. She then continued to go busily through the packets of film. I was a little astounded, but luckily I saw a third attendant and walked over and asked if he could serve me. He did.

If this store had both a customer service awareness program and a Quick and Easy Kaizen system, I am sure that the attendants would have found a way to get their own job done and to serve also the customer. Occasionally, maybe too often, people just forget the reason that the store is in business. It is to serve customers, for it is the customers that eventually pay their salaries and keeps the store in business.

If we shift the focus just slightly to find new ways to please customers, I am sure you can come up with many small Kaizens each day to improve service and also please employees at the same time.

In this store, for example, you might install a little detector that would cause a bell to sound and alert everyone in the store that a customer has entered. It is the time to smile, greet, and thank our customer for shopping with us.

Exhibit 11-1 Kaizen installed at a Camera store

Before improvement:	After improvement:
Customers would enter the store unnoticed.	Installed a simple sensor to ring a bell every time a customer enters the store.
Effect: All store employees now know when a customer enters. **Submitted By**: N. B.	

Creating is Difficult. Utilizing or Using Existing Functions is a Small Change

"You cannot hope to build a better world without improving the individuals. To that end, each of us must work for our own improvement and, at the same time, share a general responsibility for all humanity, our particular duty being to aid those to whom we think we can be most useful."
Marie Curie

Somehow, in spite of all of what we teach and say, many people continue to think that Kaizen means to only create something new. However, these days there are many convenient Kaizens we can do with things already available in our work environment. Therefore, we create something from scratch. All we have to do is to fully utilize the things around us. Take a look around you. What can you see that isn't being fully utilized?

Kaizen also means to use already existing functions

Function utilization is a typical way you can apply Kaizen in the workplace that does not create products. In our work, there are many troublesome things or cumbersome, inconvenient things. They can be as simple as a printer that wastes paper or a wastepaper basket located too far away to be useful. Those people who don't do Kaizen suffer continuously. They have to endure these inconveniences with their patience and labor. On the other hand, people who are good at Kaizen will try to find a better way of doing things, maybe by using the functions that already exist but are not being used.

For example, if your telephone number and fax number are similar, you may answer the phone and hear a fax tone fairly frequently. In this case, the sender is obviously using the wrong number. In one office, they had an extension system for their phones that included a function to forward calls to another number, just by pushing a key. One day someone thought about this. "If the telephone calls can be transferred, maybe we can transfer a fax using the same mechanism." The next time it happened, that person tried forwarding a fax call to the assigned fax number. By doing that, the fax message was transferred to the fax machine.

This particular Kaizen simply uses the existing system to transfer faxes coming in to the wrong number. It was as simple as that. This small idea completely changed the situation. It solved both the inconvenience of answering calls and getting a fax tone, and not receiving the fax.

Exhibit 11-2 Kaizen by using existing function

Before Improvement	After Improvement
Receiving fax information many times on the telephone and having to listen to the uncomfortable tone.	Transfer the call to the fax machine using the extension number system.

The Effect: By transferring you know who is sending the message and you can now receive the fax on the right machine.

Of course, if you don't already have a transfer system and you need to install one, then that would more complicated. A layperson cannot do it; telephone company specialists have to do that. However, using the existing system is not that difficult. All you need to do is think about it and be aware. Maybe a fax can be transferred. You need to study the manual and discover ways to transfer, or you can ask someone more knowledgeable. These are things anyone can do. Kaizen is something like this. You don't need special talent, or ability, or qualifications. Anybody can do it. That is Kaizen.

Another example of function utilization you can see is in office automation, especially in the personal computer field. Recent personal computers have advanced in both software and hardware. There are many functions installed. However, how many of those functions are used in day-to-day life? Not many! The advancement of functions is so rapid that the average user cannot keep up. That is reality. These functions are not fully utilized and we are

232

expending unnecessary labor and time and making unnecessary mistakes.

If we can change the situation by discovering that the computer can do this and that, we can use it in different, better ways. **If you discover one new function, fully utilize it, and apply it to your job. That is Kaizen.**

Discovering how to use all of the features of Microsoft Word to make my work easier is Kaizen. I have been working with Microsoft Word for years without ever taking the time to learn all of the features. I either thought I knew it all or that I would learn about the features when I needed them. But I was "stupid." In the past, many times, I would type away and then for seemingly no reason that I could understand I would lose a block of information; it would just disappear. Of course, I was frustrated and I would take a deep breath and then try to go back and reconstruct what I had just lost. Believe it or not but I didn't know that the little arrow on the bar, the undo arrow would bring me back to the last page or previous version before the block disappeared. Crazy! As a person who was president of a company called Productivity, Inc., you might be shocked to hear that I've lost countless hours in front of the computer because I did not know about that simple feature. It is crazy, but true.

But now with a new Kaizen mindset, each week I take out the time to learn more about each of the features in Microsoft Word, Excel, PowerPoint, etc. and that is Kaizen. I am finding new ways to make shortcuts and improve my work.

Observe, watch what employees do during the day. See what functions they use and then set up a class for them to share and learn from each other.

Kaizen through information utilization

Whether it is hardware or software, creating new functions is very difficult. It requires the knowledge and skills of a specialist. However, it is not that difficult to use the functions once the specialist has developed them. What we can do is maybe read the manuals or reference books, or ask someone who is very knowledgeable. In a way, function utilization or system utilization means Kaizen through information, or Kaizen through information utilization.

Of course, the information here may come from outside the company, or it can also be internal information. And sometimes, we might need to become aware of how to use this information.

Solving waiting time

"Slow! Is this computer really working?"

Is the computer working?

"I know the machine is working as I can see the hour glass."

I got it!

Some computer programs show an image of an hourglass to reduce frustration when the machine is doing something. When you see the hourglass, you wait. That is the effect.

We want to examine more closely all of the functions available to us to learn how to find them and use them. As an example, do you know how to use the Microsoft Word Tracking Changes feature? They helped us edit this book.

Quick & Easy KAIZEN	
Before Improvement	**After Improvement**

The effect:

Date: **Name:**

Kaizen also Means to fully Use Convenient Systems or Services

"As soon as you have made a
thought, laugh at it."
Lao-Tzu

The typical way of doing Kaizen, which is similar to function utilization, is system utilization. In the past, the only system you could use to send a package was the postal service. But today we have many different ways of sending packages: Federal Express, United Parcel (UPS), and others. There also are many different trucking companies. You can sometimes specify delivery times or have return service included. You can even send frozen items or take advantage of any variety of services offered nowadays. By using these services, you can send your items speedily, safely, and directly to the recipient. This also means Kaizen.

Of course, if you have to install a trucking system, that would be very difficult. It requires a tremendous investment. However, just to use the already existing system is not that difficult. You can study the pamphlets and brochures and listen to their explanations and learn what services they provide. If you study, you will also find unused services that you can utilize within your company. This is also Kaizen.

Exhibit 11-3 Kaizen with existing service

Before improvement	After improvement
Operators did not know how to import files into e-mails	Taught operators how to import files into e-mails and then send them
Effect: Operators can now send e-mails with attached files **Submitted By**: Dianne	

You Can Make an Improvement by Using Supporting Tools or Jigs

"There is a great satisfaction in building
good tools for other people to use."
Freeman Dyson

Another typical example of Kaizen, besides function utilization or system utilization, is utilization of supporting tools and jigs (devices for holding tools).

By using some simple tools that are already available to you, you can do your job more competently and safely, and that is Kaizen. Oftentimes it is said "humans are animals that use tools." Therefore, tool utilization is the most fundamental Kaizen for us human beings. By utilizing jigs, we can also make our work go more smoothly. Let us use the example of a Kaizen done by a student part-time employee at a large hardware store. He was working at the cash register. He was finding it very cumbersome to put the large items into the plastic bag, and he could not do it very well. If the items were small then it was no problem. But sometimes customers purchased big products that were difficult to get into the plastic bag. He had to hold the item with both hands and couldn't figure out how to open the plastic bag?

He could sometimes ask for help. But at busy times this wasn't practical. When he couldn't do it smoothly, the customers got frustrated. So, to do his job better, the student came up with the idea of using an assisting tool in the shape of an "s" (an s-hook) and he put the hook into some clay at the edge of the checkout counter. Then he put the big plastic bag onto the hook and by pull-

239

ing the other end of the bag he opened the bag wide. He then managed to put the large items more easily into the bag.

Of course it was a simple step, but that student's idea is not something to be taken too lightly. In fact, some world-renown companies are now using this idea also—you've probably seen it yourself. The world's number one toy store, Toys-R-Us, has a hook installed at the counter so that one person can handle the big items easily. In fact, they have two hooks that can slide back and forth as they choose the appropriate bag size for the item being purchased. By doing that, Toys-R-Us serves their customers very effectively.

It is not easy to pack large items

A simple hook holds one end of the bag open

My workdays used to be so intense. I would forget things and that would add even more stress to my day. In fact, I would often wake up around 2:00 AM thinking about some item I should have done the previous day. Luckily, one day I saw my partner working at his desk on his to-do list, and I then sat down and tried to copy what he was doing. I didn't have a to-do list at the time. After that moment, the to-do list became my lifesaver. I started to write down everything, every idea, every appointment, and every project, anything that I had to remember to do. I put notes on the back of the to-do list during the day. I jot down anything and everything new that pops into my mind. And it works, keeping a to-do list has helped me become a more effective manager and also to be a much calmer person in my life.

My old to-do list

Believe me, I no longer wake up startled at 2:00 AM.

Now, at the beginning of each day I look at my to-do list, which I keep on the computer. I remove the items taken care of and I type in the new items. Then I prioritize all of these for the coming day. I then print the list for "today's to-do's," and continue to jot down ideas during the day.

When I was younger, I was always forgetting things. Once I worked in New York City, but lived 35 miles away in New Rochelle, New York. My wife telephoned me earlier in the day to remind me to pick up my five-year-old daughter, Phillis, after work. She was at her grandmother's home, also in New York City. After a long hard day at the office, I left and it took me about 90 minutes to drive home. I approached the front door of my house and took one look at my wife's face to realize that I had left my daughter in New York. I turned around quickly and drove back to New York City to bring my daughter home.

What I needed was some Kaizen. I needed a mechanism to remind me, an alarm on my watch, or an alarm set on my palm computer. Often I just put a little note on my steering wheel to remind me to do things. I also carefully updated my to-do list with all of my personal things to do.

Each day I also file the old to-do list for reference. It is a great record of my activities for that day. On many occasions, I've had to go back and refer to the list.

The Idea Generator – Quick and Easy Kaizen

Prioritized To Do List: Friday, April 06, 2001

Item	Description
01	Review P73, 82, 86, 46-14B
02	Call Jack, 714-875-5668
03	Need airline tickets to Chicago
04	Pay bills, print newsletter
05	Call Mark: 514-225-1153, review contract
06	Write to subscribers on 3 courses
07	Prepare postcard mailing
09	Edit manual

Over the years I continually revise the list, change it to be more useful for me. Only last week I completely did it over again. I feel my to-do list is my most powerful business asset.

Quick & Easy KAIZEN	
Before Improvement	**After Improvement**

The effect:

Date: **Name:**

Summary

1. Kaizen is not just for the workplace where they make products. For example, Kaizen is a great tool to improve customer service. Kaizen means to select methods to accomplish your job objectives faster and better. In other words, Kaizen means to change the way you do your job.

2. Kaizen also means to better communicate, to do better calculations, and make better explanations. That is Kaizen too.

3. You can come up with many small Kaizens each day to improve service and also please employees at the same time.

Chapter 12: Sharing Kaizen Examples

"Moreover, they tend to believe that truly creative individuals are few and far between. We believe the opposite. We all have a creative side, and it can flourish if you spawn a culture to encourage it, one that embraces risks and wild ideas and tolerates the occasional failure. We've seen it happen."

Tom Kelley with Jonathan Littman
authors of The Art of Innovation

Promotion of Shortcuts through Sharing Kaizen Examples

What benefit does surfacing Kaizen bring to the company? It brings shortcuts, it brings new and better ways of doing things, which makes work easier and helps to reduce the number of unnecessary things we do. That is very easy to understand. When we share our improvement activities with each other we can understand that we aren't the only ones that need to make improvements, that others have also found things that can be improved. By sharing our Kaizens, we are proudly confessing and advertising that, in a way.

By sharing Kaizen memos, people naturally recognize that everybody has opportunities to improve. When you write down a Kaizen, you can either think, "I did such a wonderful Kaizen! I am smart!" or you can think, "The way I was doing things before was not very smart."

But by considering both viewpoints, everyone can look at the actual situation of the workplace squarely. They think they can face the reality found around them. However, in companies who are not surfacing Kaizen, they are not really recognizing their reality.

For example, the higher-ups in the organization in your own workplace might ask employees, "How are you doing?" with no real concern behind it. Many managers just don't want any more problems presented to them, so people learn to just say, "Everything is fine."

Is everything OK?

It is like when you go to a restaurant and the waiter or waitress hurries by and asks, "Is everything OK?" They really want you to say that everything is fine and so often you say, "Yes, everything is fine," even when there's a fly in your soup and you've waited forty minutes for your entrée. So in that kind of company or situation there is no atmosphere allowing you to say honestly, "We have a problem."

"Is everything OK?"
"Everything is fine."

Ask yourself, "Do they really want to know about my problems?"

If you start to talk about a problem, you will inevitably feel pressure to not say anything. So you end up saying, "We are doing fine! The soup is fantastic!" Or at work you might say, "We are working very hard. Everything is fine!"

The Idea Generator – Quick and Easy Kaizen

On a recent flight on American Airlines, as a frequent flyer, I was lucky to be upgraded to first class. But the steward was very forgetful. I asked for water and he forgot to bring it. I asked to have the salad dressing be put on the side and he forgot. Now, I realize the airplane is a very busy place with many customers to serve, but when you have the privilege of flying first class you do expect the standard for service to be the highest. American should have a system that can give the best "one-to-one" service.

We all do forget sometimes, but if we want to be noted for delivering superior customer service then we want to minimize forgetting. You can tell people in your own workplace, "You shouldn't forget!" Or you could even tell them, "Keep a list so that you will not forget." But it is far better for them to be alerted of a problem and then ask them to do a Kaizen that will prevent them from forgetting. Have them write down their ideas, test them out, share them with others and then see that the improvement process takes place.

Atmosphere that blocks Kaizen process.

Everyone stays quiet

If you work in an atmosphere like that, and you don't change the way you are doing your work, you have to cover up the problems and just do hard work. "Everything is fine!" But that kind of strenuous work doesn't last long. There is usually a breakdown of power somewhere along the way and a higher rate of turnover.

However, if you are in an environment where Kaizen memos are used, those things that may be troubling you are surfaced every time, and in a positive and constructive way. You are not complaining, you are saying, "This was a problem, and I figured out a way to fix it." Then, in spite of your "confession," others know that you are working hard and for positive change. They know that humans make mistakes, and they know that humans can learn from them too.

A mistake is a jewel; it is an opportunity to learn how to improve. It is natural to get tired and have simple misunderstandings, or to forget to turn off the lights, and so forth. Through Kaizen, everyone in the workplace can recognize that, by changing the way they do something, they can reduce that kind of potential for mistakes. When Kaizens are shared, everyone can think about how to change those situations in their own jobs.

So instead of hiding our mistakes, we actually want to bring them forward to help us make continuous improvements in the workplace. Mistakes give us—and others around us—an opportunity to make improvements. This just changes the whole attitude around us. Next time, instead of saying "Everything's fine," try shouting out, "I found a jewel! Isn't it wonderful? Now I can do another Kaizen!" Or you can at least think it to yourself.

"The brain learns from making mistakes!"
Dr. Dee Tadlock

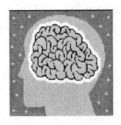

Dr. Dee Tadlock, President of Read Right Systems, Inc. has developed a new method to teach children and adults how to read. The new method is based on her extensive research that shows the brain really learns from making mistakes. The brain creates new neural networks from finding new solutions to mistakes. Imagine the concept: the brain learns from making mistakes!

Dr. Tadlock's method taught my grandson Sam how to read in just three months. When Sam started in the first grade he was the worst reader in his class. At the end of that school year he could not read at all. But today, five years later, he is the best reader in his entire school. In fact, Sam, now in the sixth grade, reads at a college level.

Sam's brain was reprogrammed during those three months. He was taught to pursue excellence in his reading. He would listen to an excellent reader, either my daughter reading to him or to a tape recorder. After listening several times, Sam would then read the paragraph. He kept repeating this process over and over again until his brain, learning from his mistakes, finally was able to read the paragraph out loud almost perfectly. Then and only then could Sam go on to the next paragraph.

Sadly, so many children and adults suffer unnecessarily from not being able to read. This wonderful process developed by Dr. Tadlock might prove that our entire school system is upside down. Generally, students are punished for making mistakes, so they try to hide them.

I remember loving kindergarten. And then something happened in the first grade to change the way I felt about school. I was given tests in the first grade and learned how "dumb" I was. Points were taken away from me on my tests because of the mistakes I made. The teachers did not understand that my brain learns from making mistakes!

There might be many people in your company suffering from misconceptions they internalized from their past teachers. And the terror generated from our school systems about making mistakes could be carried over into the workplace. Many of your employees could feel embarrassed and be doing their best to hide their mistakes; they might not be comfortable participating in a Quick and Easy Kaizen process, especially if they have trouble reading or writing. But you have the power to change that.

Kaizen encourages positive thinking.

Quick and Easy Kaizen supports the idea that revealing and correcting mistakes will advance your own aims and the aims of your company.

Kaizen activities are brain exercises.

We want to reveal the root causes of your problems so that you can address them and get rid of them, one by one. And, don't worry, there will always be other things to find and correct—and improve!

By looking at case studies and real life examples, everyone can learn how to change their own situations. You can see that just changing the steps, for example, can make a job easier. Or maybe it's a change in colors, or maybe a coding system could be effective, things like that.

Kaizen examples

The Kaizen examples you collect from employees become a collection of hints for further improvements like a manual or textbook for the future. By using Kaizen examples, you share your successes and failures. By surfacing Kaizen, you share the following two things:

1. By looking at the "Before Improvement" column, you can **share your failures** and the not-so-effective ways of doing work. You are really saying "Before Kaizen, since we did such-and-such, we had many mistakes or accidents. We were frustrated and had trouble with customers." Poor ways of doing work are reported in the "Before Kaizen" part of the memo. However, Kaizen examples don't stop there.

2. You also have an "After Improvement" column. This is where you can say "By doing this, we no longer make mistakes. We are safer and more comfortable. We have happier customers," and there are better ways of doing the

work. In other words, you are **sharing your successes**. By sharing your failures and successes in your own workplace, this becomes a firmer foundation for future Kaizen improvements.

On one of our factory visits, we noticed a group of workers setting up inspection teams to look for possible things that could cause accidents such as dangling ropes, ladders, boxes, slippery floors, things too close to the heat, open doors creating drafts, etc. Instead of just waiting for problems to happen, they had formed a team to go out and look for potential accidents that might occur. Then they used Kaizen to make the necessary improvements.

A Kaizen example also compares a poor way of doing work and a better way of doing work. By looking at these comparisons many times, it gives us food for thought. Review your own work and how you are doing things, and compare it with someone else's Kaizen. Simply saying "Let's review our work" doesn't go too far without this kind of specific example because, without it, we don't know where to start. There is nothing to grab hold of and so the idea slips away.

Companies that share their Kaizen examples know that everybody has had such an experience (of doing an incorrect or even 'stupid' things). Therefore, when an employee does something careless once, the next time it is easier for him to recognize an opportunity to correct the situation and do another Kaizen.

Forced Kaizen Versus Spontaneous Kaizen

"You've got to take the initiative and play your game . . . confidence makes the difference."

Chris Evert Lloyd

When people notice problems on their own, they are more inclined to solve them on their own. But given the same problem, if someone else points it out to them, they will likely feel upset. This is a critical shortcoming of traditional suggestion systems because somebody else is making suggestions regarding "my work." Which means you are being told, "you are making mistakes, and this is a better way of doing your work." Because if you are doing an excellent job, doing your job the smart way, nobody else would make suggestions on this or that. Since you are doing something incorrectly, it is pointed out and suggested. "How about trying this way?" rarely sounds as helpful as it is intended to be.

Even when people have noticed their own mistakes, it can be upsetting when someone else mentions it. Then what happens? In your mind, that particular suggestion may be really good, but emotionally you don't want to accept it. So you create all kinds of reasons to not do it. And you could be very reluctant to implement the suggestion. However, if your boss makes the suggestion to you, you have to do it, like it or not. And that is the sad reality for many employed people.

The Idea Generator – Quick and Easy Kaizen

Even if you don't really want to do it, you have to do it. And you say, "Well, I will do it if it is the manager's order. I'll do it if they want me to. I did it since I was told to." That is Kaizen being forced on people.

Well in a way, even though it is a forced Kaizen, if it works well and your work becomes easier and more comfortable, that would still be better than no Kaizen at all.

Forced Kaizen does not have "staying power"

Kaizen does not always go smoothly, although you intend it to. Sometimes a Kaizen ends as a failure against your intentions—maybe your work becomes better, but it causes trouble to other people, etc.

What happens if that Kaizen is forced upon a worker and resentment happens? The person who is given the Kaizen or forced to do it will not be happy. "Well, my manager told me to do this, but it didn't work." Since that Kaizen was reluctantly done, the slightest problem might drive them to quit immediately. Or rather, they might anticipate some problem to occur before they even try the Kaizen and use lots of excuses—and not do it. Kaizen will never last in this kind of situation.

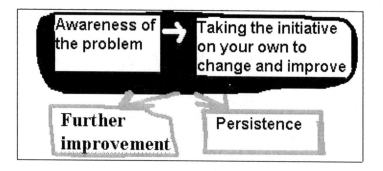

On the other hand, if the problem is something that same employee notices on her own, and she decides to implement Kaizen, of course sometimes it may not work! However, when her Kaizen doesn't work and no one is pleased with the result, she—and most employees—probably won't quit that easily. She will wonder why? Why did that happen? How about trying it this way? And to a certain extent she will become more persistent.

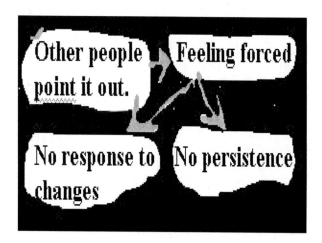

Then the principles of Kaizen implementation start to kick in: attack by changing viewpoints, attack by changing the level of actions. Kaizen does not guarantee success with the first try. **Try it, and if it doesn't work try Kaizen again. And if that doesn't**

256

work, make another Kaizen! That cycle has to repeat. Kaizen requires persistence.

Where does persistence come from? It begins with your awareness. If you notice your own problem, if you take the initiative to start doing a Kaizen, you can have that persistence to pursue the idea until positive change results. But if somebody else points out the problem and you feel forced to do the Kaizen, you do it reluctantly and it will lack persistence.

Learn from your own examples, and teach others from your own examples—until they at last begin to learn from theirs. By recognizing your own improvement needs and spontaneous Kaizen ideas, and sharing them with others, you immediately dissolve the negative undertones that can sometimes poison a Kaizen system.

Be careful you don't fall into this kind of thinking instead: "If I suggest an improvement people resent it. If I don't say anything it just doesn't get improved!" We've heard well-meaning managers say, "I know that principle. I know that theory. It is true that people do not like to have their own problems pointed out to them. Therefore, as a manager, I try not to criticize my subordinates. I try not to give detailed points, because I don't want to be disliked by my subordinates. I try to wait until they notice the problems themselves and try to take the initiative on their own. I encourage them. I try to make them feel that way. But they are not sensitive enough to make those small changes on their own. No matter how long I wait, they don't notice their problems and then I can no longer wait. I don't want to have an accident or problems with customers. Therefore, there is no choice but for me to point out their problems. But if I point out the problems, they become upset and speak up. But if I don't do it, they don't notice the problem. I don't want to do this, but since I don't say it, they don't notice. What should I do?"

Sharing leads to your own awareness	
Quick & Easy KAIZEN	
Before Improvement	*After Improvement*
We are doing funny things	Change
The effect: We reduced problems	
Date:	Name:

Granted, it is disconcerting to any manager to be aware of a problem and simply stand by, trusting someone else will take care of it. But, by having problems pointed out people become upset. And if it is not pointed out they might not notice the error! What should we do? Well...

What should we do?

This will probably be a common feeling among managers who have one or more people working for them. Actually, the compilation of Kaizen examples can help solve this problem. The compilation of case examples is distributed to the people in the workplace as objective information. Therefore, since it is objective information, and it is another person's Kaizen. You don't take it personally. You feel detached in seeing other workers' Kaizens. And you soon recognize that we all make similar mistakes. Likewise, we are all finding better ways to get our jobs done.

Nevertheless, most companies are sure to have some people who will look at the other people's Kaizens and think, "Doing

258

something like that is really stupid. If they did it from the begin-ning that way (the way they have improved it), they wouldn't have had any problems at all. This is so obvious. It should be done, naturally. It is common sense. Who is this stupid guy who had been doing these stupid things? Oh that is department such-and-such. That group has lots of stupid people," or something like that. They will become detached from seeing other people's examples

When mistakes are made, some people will always try to look for someone else to blame. "It is the other department's fault. They should have done it differently!" You might also hear these people ask, "Why don't they do something about it? Or why don't they just do something to fix that?" Well, wouldn't life be a lot easier if we could all just figure out who "they" are? We would have no more responsibilities, would we? But in Kaizen, we do what we can. And when a mistake happens we look around and see what "we" can do to fix it.

When you read examples of Kaizen in other companies, it is like looking at a mirror into your own workplace; your own work-place examples are inevitably shown there too. Then maybe you will notice that you are also doing something that can be done dif-ferently. And when you realize it on your own, then that becomes a base for further improvement in your workplace.

What if the Kaizen compilation borrowed from other places does not work or isn't useful?

To gain anything from the Kaizen compilation, your company has to have its own Kaizen examples. If they are your own com-pany's Kaizen examples, then noticing that incident will convince you—will convince the many workers at your place of business

259

too. Even if a similar example is given in the other company's Kaizen, of course those people who understand well can translate that Kaizen to their own work situation and apply them and notice the shortcomings of their work. But those people who do not understand it that well say, "that is a different industry, different type of job, different situation," and they don't connect the example to their own work. They don't get it. Fortunately we have many Kaizen examples around us. We are talking about small changes, and small changes are abundant in our day-to-day work. If only the opportunity to make big changes is possible for us, then it is really difficult to change any one thing. Big change examples are often sited from other companies' examples or from famous examples. They are interesting stories, but most people say that is aside from their job. They have their own job, and there are interesting stories out there but they are not always helpful to make changes. They are someone else's problem, not mine.

But Kaizen should not be that way. Kaizen examples are within their day-to-day work. Therefore, Kaizen examples are completely applicable to their work. By looking at these examples, they will understand. Kaizen and work arc not separate things; they are the same thing.

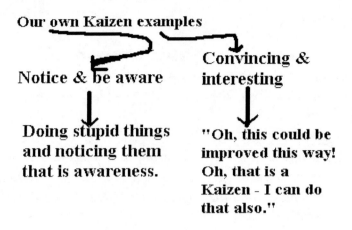

Once I was managing a data processing company in the Island of Grenada in the West Indies. We were given a very large project from the New York Telephone Company. At first when I looked at the work I thought it would be impossible to do. I could hardly understand it myself. How was I going to teach the staff to do the work? I thought that to do it you really needed a college education—but not one person of the 150 in the room had attended a college. But as it is said,

> *"Necessity is the mother of our invention."*
> **Plato, *The Repulic***

I didn't have a choice. We either had to do this job and do it well or we would have to shut the business down. Magically a thought came into my head that said, "This job is also being done in Jamaica and if they can do it so can we!"

I then gathered all the people together and told them of my reservation—and also that if the people in Jamaica could do it so *could they. I challenged both them and myself. I told them we needed a miracle.*

Well, a miracle came. Slowly we all began to understand the requirements of the job and we did it and did it so successfully that we continued to serve the telephone company for the next ten years.

What really saved us was knowing that someone else had accomplished the same thing. This removed all our reservations and gave us the charge and the energy we needed to accomplish that task successfully.

Isn't it like many sports activities, for example, track and field? When someone sets a world record, everyone else has something to shoot for. We know what has been done and so now we can make our plans to improve to the best we can. Maybe we can break a world record, or maybe we will just have fun trying to continuously improve.

We know that Dana Corporation does it well. We know that thousands of Japanese companies do it well. We know you can do it well.

262

Quick and Easy Kaizen Sharing

*"Talent is always conscious of its own
abundance, and does not object to sharing."*
Alexander Solzhenitsyn

After you implement your Kaizen, it's important to follow up or simply write it down so that it can surface for everyone else to see. If you say you will do a Kaizen, then write down the Kaizen you plan to do, but if you do not follow through, Kaizen activity will not continue or take root in your organization.

If you just stop there, after writing it down, then that doesn't accomplish much either. In other words, don't write it and then do nothing, and don't collect other people's Kaizen forms and do nothing. That is nothing but a waste of paper.

Writing Kaizen reports is the beginning of surfacing. But to complete the cycle, they must also be fed back into the system immediately, and shared among people.

Often when we talk about sharing Kaizen, people's reactions are just to compile Kaizen examples at the promotion office. Of course it is important to compile these documents. However, the most important feedback should be done right there at the workplace.

Since we are talking about day-to-day Kaizen activity, feedback should also be on a day-to-day basis. Otherwise, it doesn't have much value.

The company-wide Kaizen compilation may be shared quarterly or every half-year. This large compilation does not take the place, however, of day-to-day feedback. Because we do work everyday, and Kaizen is done everyday, some level of **Kaizen feedback should also be given everyday.** For example, if your workplace has a morning meeting, the new Kaizen should be introduced at the meeting. If you have a work report meeting, then work improvement reporting should be done at the same time.

Some companies have three-minute speeches from each member each morning. In such a company employees often feel it is burdensome. They worry, "Tomorrow I have to speak at the meeting. I have to say something profound or witty," and they think and think and try to discover something to say. However, a speech, which doesn't really connect to the work at hand, is not very significant. It is better to share your own, personal Kaizen.

Since Kaizen can be written out in three minutes, it can also be shared in three minutes, even if you speak slowly. And **presenting a mini-report like this, on a daily basis, makes Kaizen activity continue in the workplace;** doing so ensures that Kaizen becomes a part of your daily work.

3 Essential Steps of Kaizen:

1. **Just saying is no good for the value of Kaizen is in implementation.**

2. **Just implementing is not good enough. You must write it down to surface the Kaizen to reveal what you did.**

3. Just collecting written Kaizen memos is not good enough. You must share the Kaizens with others to create an environment for continuous improvement.

Sharing Examples in Your Facility's Newsletter

"Life is not easy for any of us. But what of that? We must have perseverance and above all confidence in ourselves. We must believe that we are gifted for something and that this thing must be attained."

Marie Curie

Of course, sharing Kaizen should be done not only in each office or division, but also across the company as a whole. However, it doesn't mean that you need to make a very thick compilation of Kaizen examples. We are talking about simple Kaizen. Therefore, it is not really suitable to develop a big, impressive Kaizen book. If it is a big book, it cannot be shared quickly and easily.

A better method is to have a newsletter, like *Kaizen News*, which introduces two or three Kaizen examples a month. To that extent, Kaizens can be shared quickly and easily.

Kaizen News

Newsletter

The Idea Generator – Quick and Easy Kaizen

After you have produced a year or two of newsletters, then maybe you can just put a cover on it and that becomes an excellent compilation of Kaizen examples. This really materializes the major principles of Kaizen: showing details of small improvement ideas.

The most effective way to share information is to break it down and present it many times, quickly and easily. A thick book of Kaizen examples, which takes lots of money and time to create, is almost of no value because nobody would read such a big book. And usually those thick books will be stored away in the cabinet or desk drawer and that is very wasteful.

Simple Presentation Meeting

The same thing is true of a presentation. It is really nonsensical to spend much effort and time to prepare such a presentation meeting. A Kaizen presentation should also be given in a relaxed manner, quickly and easily. To prepare for a presentation, you don't have to make a lot of overhead transparencies. At the minimum, what you will need are two overhead transparencies. One is to show "Before Kaizen" and one is "After Kaizen."

This overhead presentation can be **a powerful catalyst for change.** While people are presenting their problems and their solutions, it also allows others to comment, to ask questions, and to make suggestions on how additional improvements can be done.

Also, there is no need to practice for this kind of presentation. Don't worry about any form of criticism; just keep it simple, quick and easy. In short, only three points need to be explained. What is it? How did you do it? What happened? The best presentation is no-frills. Maybe just simple and candid, that is the best.

I have visited many companies that do have Kaizen activities. At many of the plants and offices, I would ask if they would please show me some examples of their Kaizens. I remember being introduced to workers who came up with the idea and I can still clearly see the excitement and pride in their faces as they showed me their ideas. One man particularly showed me how he created a device that would absolutely prevent him from making a mistake. He was forced to pick up parts in their exact sequence. His Kaizen prevented him from inadvertently or forgetfully picking up a part out of sequence. As he showed me his Kaizen his face was all a glow. I understood at that moment, and others like it, the real power of the Kaizen system.

The Idea Generator – Quick and Easy Kaizen

Examples from New United Motor Manufacturing, Inc. (NUMMI):

1. **Problem:** Excess cost. Four cab mounts on each truck requires total of 8 bolts at 11 cents each.

    Solution: Use bolts of same strength and length used on the gas tanks costing 7.5 cents each.

    Result: Savings of 28 cents per vehicle, annually 151,098 vehicles at .28 cents is a savings of $42,307.44.

    By: Debi Moniz and Arlene D. Martinez

2. **Problem:** Assortment of plastic electrical connector, dust, and valve covers are removed and thrown away – costly and not biodegradable hurting the environment.

    Solution: Send reusable caps and covers back to suppliers for reuse.

    Effect: Protection of the environment

    By: Debi Moniz and Arlene D. Martinez

3. **Problem:** Stud on vehicle has a cotter keyhole but cotter key is no longer used.

Solution: Replace struts with a less expensive stud without the drilled hole.

Effect: Annual estimated savings is $330,240.00 per year

By: Debi Moniz and Arlene D. Martinez

We are looking for small ideas, and the above are small ideas, but sometimes small ideas can have very big effects.

Kaizen Seminar

"The reward of work is more work,
it is the increased capacity to perform."
Rudi

On the previous page we showed some simple Kaizen examples that had a very big effect. And some companies tend to have a very elaborate presentation system and tend to select only high-level Kaizen examples to teach the system. We would discourage you from presenting Kaizen this way. It is not such a good idea to feature things like the President's Award or the Kaizen which saved the company $10,000. Yes, a $10,000 cost savings is important but for your Kaizen education effort it can have a negative effect. Because such high-level Kaizen is too high-level and too specialized for those people who are outside that department, there is a good chance they won't understand and it might be intimidating to them.

Instead of promoting examples that few workers can relate to, you should create a presentation that everybody can understand. The last thing you want to do is present the high-level Kaizen examples that can intimidate the participants by implying, "To be in this organization, we have to be that good." Therefore, the more you elaborate your presentation session, the less participation you are likely to see in Kaizen

One company had such a bad experience that it decided to make a big change in how it conducts presentation sessions. They selected ten examples, and among those ten eight were small, simple, easy to understand, interesting Kaizen. That accounts for

80%. Then each presenter's method of presentation was changed dramatically. In the years before "the change," the presenters tended to talk a lot in detail. When you present simple Kaizens, if you just show transparencies on the screen, everybody "gets it" just by doing that. So the presentation will be very short and they say, "Well, that's it!" and it's no big deal.

And every time each presenter finishes, the President of the company stands up and says, "It is very important to have such Kaizens" and makes a comment. Then they may say, "You say it is no big deal, but until that time we have not even practiced that simple thing, and by neglecting that we have neglected our customers." But because of the Kaizen you have made, we no longer have to worry about that, and that is excellent," and they will follow-up on the Kaizen like that.

Therefore, the main emphasis of Kaizen activity should be small Kaizens. A presentation session in which the bulk of the presentation is small Kaizens makes small Kaizens the main focus. However, many managers and bosses like to show off the ideas from their workers. They take pride in the idea that "their" employees were so clever. **But, sometimes when the boss tells his boss about it, the praise goes to the boss instead of to the worker. It is better when you ask the worker to explain their Kaizen to visitors, to others that come into the work place.**

Also, a presentation is not real sharing if there are only difficult Kaizens discussed. The person watching the presentation says, "I don't understand at all. That's not related to us. It would be impossible for us to do such a big Kaizen." Simple Kaizen makes the presentation also simple. Printed, this small Kaizen is not a big deal. It is a very tiny Kaizen. It is really ordinary. But it is easy to understand. And people say, "To that extent, I can do it too."

Three items for Kaizen seminar

1. **What**
2. **Why**
3. **How**

Meanwhile, the work continues to grow. Do you want to manage it with your labor or with your ingenuity?

Let's look back and review things. Three things: Kaizen implementation, surfacing Kaizen, and sharing Kaizen. And we talked about three steps. What. Why. How.

In the first part of the book, we discussed what Kaizen is. In the second part, we explained the Kaizen steps, principles or rules through practical and complete examples. At the same time, we discussed the effectiveness of Kaizen, or for whom we do Kaizen: whether Kaizen is to your benefit or your loss. In this third part, we have been presenting the Quick and Easy Kaizen memo methods and also we discussed how to share Kaizen examples. We also repeatedly discussed the necessity of surfacing and sharing Kaizen.

We would like to emphasize here, again, that when you explain for whom you do Kaizen, it is important to use your own complete examples. **If you use your own complete examples that everybody can associate with, it is easy for them to understand that Kaizen is really for them.**

Even after understanding that it is to you're own benefit, there are people who will say, "I understand that my work can become easier by doing Kaizen. But as soon as my job gets easier, I will be given another task to do. By doing that, there is no end to it. It means I will lose in the long run by doing Kaizen."

In each workplace there are people who are bound to think like that. Our answer to such individuals is "**the nature of our job is to get better.**" It is not because the company is mean and wants to punish those who do Kaizen and make their jobs easier. Whether you do Kaizen or not, regardless, the company hopes the volume of work will continue to grow. But, because of the slow economy, the company is faced with the fact that it might have to reduce the workforce. This really has nothing to do with whether the company does Kaizen or not. Hopefully, as your company becomes more efficient they also become more competitive.

To survive and prevail in this competitive world, we have to meet the ever-increasing demand of the customer. In other words, we have to do more than what we are doing now. Whether it is a good economy or sluggish economy, the volume of work per person continues to grow. That is an absolute condition for a company to continue to exist. If the quantity of work per person continues to decrease, then that company cannot survive.

If you just look at Wall Street and the stock market, you will see that it is the growth companies that are the most appealing. It is necessary that we all look to grow, as companies and as individuals.

Work smarter not (only) harder

Therefore, the volume of work will continue to increase. We have to keep up with it. To do that, there are two choices. One is to keep up through labor. Two is through our ingenuity. Of course it is okay to keep up with an increasing job through labor—working harder not smarter. But it has a limit. People cannot continue to work 24 hours a day. The better choice is to devise a way to do the job better, either through automation or through Kaizen.

As we said earlier, in 1776, 97% of the American populace was farmers. Today, it takes only three people out of 100 to feed the rest of us. If we didn't improve our agricultural process, imagine what our lives would be like today?

Valuable Labor and Labor with No Value

Of course, we are not saying that all problems can be solved with Kaizen. There are many constraints. Therefore, we have problems that cannot be solved by Kaizen. In such a case, we have to cope with the situation with labor or through our efforts. But that is valuable effort. It is meaningless to put a lot of effort into doing things, which can be done easily by changing the method a little bit. That is effort with no value.

Rather than putting a lot of effort into those things that have no value, it is better to devise a way to do it easier and put the time and energy saved through that Kaizen into more valuable efforts. And that is what adds more value to your work and adds value to your life. We have precious little time in our lives. Which is more beneficial to you? Putting that time towards valuable things or things of little value? This is the fundamental reason we do Kaizen.

Somehow, we all must work smarter and continuously grow. Kaizen is a wonderful tool to help us grow.

> **After Kaizen, our work becomes easier.**
>
> **Then a new job is given to us.**
> **Work increases in terms of quantity and quality.**
>
> **Keep up through labor or ingenuity?**

The workforce today continues to reduce and the workload continues to increase. Without Kaizen, you have to put more effort or labor into it. Difficult problems require valuable labor. You should invest your effort in creating valuable work and a valuable life. Do not waste your effort on work with no value. If you have labor with no value, then solve it by ingenuity and eliminate unnecessary labor and effort. Use your energy for important things.

Kaizen means to devise a way so that you can do ordinary things well. We have many problems because the actual situation in our work environment is such that the way it should be done is not the way it is always done. Therefore, strong companies know that to do the ordinary things well, they need to have Kaizen company-wide.

Therefore, strong companies make an effort to develop company-wide Kaizen activity so that they can do ordinary things well and continue to do that. Quick and Easy Kaizen can stimulate people to really grow on the job. It allows them to offer improvement ideas and then to learn new skills to develop themselves to implement those ideas.

I remember visiting a steel mill where a worker came up with an idea to reduce the loss of heat when doors were opened as the hot steel was moved from area to area. He wanted to install a simple hot air curtain in front of the door to prevent heat from escaping, but he did not have the electrical skills to make the change. His supervisor liked the idea and instead of getting an electrician to install the change he asked an electrician to teach the worker how to do the wiring himself. Imagine how the worker felt when he himself installed his own idea. What a wonderful way to grow!

Summary

1. **Sharing Kaizen examples:**

   - **Before Kaizen = mistakes, poor way of doing things.**
   - **After Kaizen = success, better way of doing things.**
   - **Sharing mistakes and successes.**
   - **By sharing Kaizen examples, it can lead to the next cycle of Kaizen.**

2. **Compilation of Kaizen examples includes:**

   - **Poor way of doing work.**
   - **Better way of doing work.**
   - **A hint for reviewing, inspecting your way of doing your job. It is a wonderful starting point.**

3. **"If I suggest an improvement, people resent it. If I don't say anything it just doesn't get improved!"**

4. **When looking at Kaizen examples:**

   - **Think about what method we can do.**
   - **Think of a way we can do it.**

5. If it doesn't work try Kaizen again. That cycle has to be repeated. Kaizen requires persistence.

6. When looking at borrowed examples be careful:

    - Think about the reasons why we cannot do it.
    - Why do you get upset, or show indifference, or show a lack of interest?
    - "Of course that company can do it! Their jobs are different. Industry, size and culture of the company are different!"

7. Kaizen reports need to be fed back into the system immediately and shared among people.

8. Kaizen is a day-to-day activity, and feedback should also be on a day-to-day basis.

9. Eliminate the unfinished:

    - Saying and not doing.
    - Doing but not doing any follow-up.
    - Writing without any follow-up.
    - Collecting but no follow-up later.

10. Sharing Kaizen reports on a daily basis in the workplace helps Kaizen activity continue.

11. Kaizen seminar basics:

    - Implementation of Kaizen
    - Surfacing Kaizen

- **Sharing Kaizen**

12. Three items for Kaizen seminar:

- **What**
- **Why**
- **How**

Chapter 13: Learning Kaizens from Other Companies

*"Character cannot be developed in ease
and quiet. Only through experience of trial
and suffering can the soul be strengthened,
ambition inspired, and success achieved."*
                                    Helen Keller

Applying Other Companies' Kaizen Examples to Your Own Work

To get the maximum benefit from this book and the material here, we do expect you to write out your own Kaizen ideas on the blank forms.

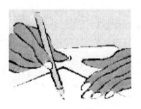

Please start writing.

When we teach a Kaizen seminar in-house, the examples are drawn from within the company. However, when we teach at a public seminar, where there are many participants from many different companies, representing different types of industries and jobs, the examples selected for the seminar are very typical, simple examples. Therefore, by just looking at those examples, oftentimes the reaction of the participants is, "Well, that's so small and trivial." If the participants have that kind of attitude, however, they cannot learn anything from the other companies, other industries' examples.

When you study examples, even the simple examples, they share the common principles or rules of Kaizen. If you can identify those principles in other companies' Kaizens and in other people's examples, then you can apply those principles and improve your own job. To do that, though, you must first train yourself to write out your own Kaizen examples. If you don't write down your own Kaizen examples, you will only get half the value of reading this book or attending a Kaizen seminar.

When I first discovered Just-in-time (JIT) in Japan in 1981, I was tickled. I was really excited to share this powerful production system with other American companies, but I had great difficulty in communicating the real importance of this system and the competitive advantages it had given Toyota and their subcontractors over other companies in the world.

But when I would speak to an audience of managers, I found they were not getting excited at all. Many said, "It wouldn't work here, we are different."

I remember visiting Boeing in Seattle around 1983, to present the JIT concepts to them. I could not rouse their interest at all. They had incredible resistance to change. Boeing was the leader in the world at manufacturing airplanes for the aviation industry, with very little competition. As world leaders they probably thought, "Why should we change our methods?" Yes, Boeing did eventually install JIT—fifteen years later. Imagine the billions of dollars Boeing lost by waiting so long.

The Idea Generator – Quick and Easy Kaizen

If you are not involved in the creative process while you read, it will be very difficult to apply the ideas or teach others. You cannot gain that much because many of the examples are from some other company, some other people's examples, not yours. Therefore, we encourage learning from other companies' examples and then applying the principles shown in their Kaizens to your own job.

It is not that hard to do this. What you need to do is think about your own situation and just use that principle to improve your work. By simply doing that, you will come to recognize the common principles in Kaizen. This is a very simple act, but there are people who do not want to do this and cannot think in these terms. There are people who find it difficult to learn from examples from other companies or different industries, so you must be prepared to give them examples from their own.

A serendipitous discovery

Jack Warne, former president of Omark Industries, traveled to Japan on my second study mission. During the first week, after visiting seven different manufacturing plants, Jack said, "My company is much better, the Japanese should come and visit me at Omark." As the leader of the mission, I was very disappointed by not being able to please Jack. But, on Tuesday of the second week we visited Nippondenso Electric, a manufacturer of air-conditioners and a Toyota Motors subcontractor. The plant manager, Mr. Ohta, demonstrated a quick change over of a punch press, which took only a few minutes. Mr. Ohta also took us to a meeting room and explained the concept of mix modeling, how to produce different products on the same manufacturing line. Finally, it all clicked in Jack's mind and he became like a child dis-

covering something new and it excited him. He discovered the power of Just-in-time (JIT).

When Jack returned to America, he asked all of his managers and engineers to study a book we found on the trip written by Dr. Shigeo Shingo, "A Study of the Toyota Production System from Industrial Engineering Viewpoint." Jack and I each bought 500 copies. The Omark managers would read one chapter at a time, in study groups, and ask the fundamental question, "How can we apply this information at Omark?"

Within a few months Omark reduced their inventory over 50%, shrinking the needed floor space in their plants to half, and went on and became the most productive American company applying JIT. Once it clicks in your mind, the changes can happen quickly.

Dell Computer can today build and ship a computer from your order in just one week. The concept of JIT might have started at Toyota, but Mr. Taiichi Ohno (the vice president and co-creator of JIT with Dr. Shingo) claimed that he learned all about JIT from Henry Ford. It seems that over the years Ford Motor Company just simply ignored or forgot the system that originally lead to its success. Well, Omark used it and then Dell used it. (Hopefully, we are getting you so excited about Quick and Easy Kaizen that you will use Omark's technique and also buy 500 copies of this book!)

There is such power in discovering from other companies, even companies outside your industry. Go visit other companies. If you like what they are doing you can always set up a little experiment to see if it works for you.

The Idea Generator – Quick and Easy Kaizen

So many people resist change and actually find a million reasons why they shouldn't do it. "Well, it sounds good, but do you know of a company exactly like ours that is doing it?" There is no company exactly like yours!

Most people resist change of any kind, but when they see something very positive happening in another company with their own eyes, it does make it easier for them to open up to the possibilities. If, for example, you work for a hospital and you read about a new x-ray machine working at another hospital, you can visit that other hospital, see it working, and ask questions. Then it becomes much easier for you to order that new x-ray machine for your hospital. It is "safe" because an organization in your industry with a successful reputation seems to be using the technology effectively—this seems to reduce the gamble in making change in your own company. However, it might work and it might not work for you.

The trick is to search for the best technology, the best management process, and not be concerned what kind of institution is using it. It doesn't have to be exactly like yours. During the 1980s, I lead around 35 study missions to Japan, and managers from various industries looked at Just-In-Time (JIT) and Total Quality Control (TQC), and they were able to take it back and use it in their companies in America. Sure it started at Toyota, an automotive company, but Proctor and Gamble was able to do it and change their production process to deliver diapers on a JIT basis to Wal-Mart. Benchmarking, seeing others do it, can really help you reduce your resistance to change and allow you to install new ideas more quickly.

Dr. Shigeo Shingo, the creator of JIT, once said that there are three kinds of problem-finding engineers:

1. NYET engineers – they always say no. It doesn't matter what you ask them, they always say it will not work here.

2. Desk engineers – they never get up and go to the factory to see what the real problem is. They only look for the solutions in their books and manuals.

3. Catalogue engineers – they only look up solutions in their catalogues so they can order the solution from somewhere else.

William Christopher, a friend and fellow author said that we should add a fourth type of engineer, the good type who designs, builds, solves problems, and creates solutions.

With Kaizen, we want to find ways to say "yes" so that we can find new solutions. We want to get up and go out and look to see the actual problem at the site, either in the factory, the office, the store, or wherever the problem occurs, and we want to find ways to solve problems without spending money—spending money is the last resort.

The Idea Generator – Quick and Easy Kaizen

Quick & Easy KAIZEN	
Before Improvement	*After Improvement*
The effect:	
Date:	**Name:**

Kaizen Welcomes Imitation

*"Not to engage in the pursuit of ideas
is to live like ants instead of men."*
Mortimer Adler

Kaizen Doesn't Question Where You Get the Idea

When you have implemented a simple, obvious Kaizen, there is another argument you might hear, especially in a company with a traditional suggestion system. "We cannot accept your idea because it has already been done in another department." However, with a Quick and Easy Kaizen system, we don't hear this kind of talk because **true Kaizen does not question where you got the idea.** Whether you thought of the Kaizen by yourself, or you got the idea from reading somebody else's Kaizen and implemented it in your own job, or you got the idea from reading the newspaper or watching television—even if someone else told you the idea, it is not questioned.

The important thing is to adapt the better method to your work and improve your work situation. That is Kaizen. Those people who are good at Kaizen are very good observers of other people's work.

> **People good at Kaizen are good at observing other people's work**

Whether the idea is applied to the same industry or a different industry, these people can look at the scenario and say, "Oh, that is an interesting way of doing things. Well, I am going to borrow that idea," and they implement it immediately.

My job for twenty years was to go to Japan and other countries to observe, to study carefully, to find, to select and publish books on their best management practices and to bring back the information to America to improve productivity, quality and customer service.

In retrospect, I think I was a very good copier.

But, somehow we often reject the idea of copying. Of course, we want people to be original and creative, and we want to be that way ourselves. But we learn first from copying. Remember when you were a child? Or look at your own children. Learning comes from observing and copying others first, then we can be original.

Stop, reduce and change

The three rules to Kaizen are: stop, reduce and change. You can add, imitate, and copy to those too. In any case, Kaizen welcomes imitation very much. If you consider it a good thing, then you should apply it to your own work more and more. That is Kaizen. Don't restrict yourself to one way of doing things. Always consider that there may be a better way or various ways to do the same thing. "Maybe other companies are no longer doing it the way we are doing it."

Of course we are not saying to copy patented ideas or those that are proprietary to the company. We are not saying that. But we can certainly learn from others.

Five years ago, The Baptist Health Care System in Pensacola, Florida, was one of the lowest-rated hospitals in America in customer service. They decided to change. They established a new vision to be the best hospital system in America, and they went and visited other hospitals with high ratings. But here's the most interesting part: they also visited manufacturing plants. They studied well, copied the best ideas, and in 1991 they were rated as one of the best hospitals in America in a study conducted by USA Today.

It is funny, but certain ideas can be patented or copyrighted and protected by law. That protects the investment of the creator and gives them a competitive advantage. But, since Kaizen is small changes, we can go out and legally borrow, and copy those wonderful ideas from others that are not patented or copyrighted, and not have to worry about all those laws and regulations.

Companies that Destroy Kaizen, and Companies that Foster Kaizen

"Change means movement. Movement means friction. Only in the frictionless vacuum of a nonexistent abstract world can movement or change occur without that abrasive friction of conflict."
Saul Alinsky

As we have discussed, Kaizen already exists here and there in any workplace. Even in any poorly performing company, you can easily find a quick example or two of Kaizen. The problem is that it doesn't last in these companies. When someone does Kaizen in an under-performing company, the reaction is generally, "That's too little, too obvious, and ordinary." And in doing so, they are destroying their own Kaizen effort.

On the other hand, stronger companies shed light on the things their employees are unconsciously doing and say "That's Kaizen!" They make a conscious effort to recognize and respect the employees' efforts, and then they encourage people to look at ways to make similar improvements. They guide employees to seek out more Kaizens, so that employees come up with more ideas and make more improvements.

One goal is to stop doing the unnecessary things you have been doing. **The time saved by not doing the unnecessary things can be used to do important, necessary things more thoroughly. That's why you can expect quality and productivity to be improved.**

291

Over time, the accumulated effort will transform into something phenomenal. Imagine the feeling that employees will have when they recognize that they are all part of the improvement effort—all part of the wonderful effect taking place. Have a party and thank them!

Companies that foster Kaizen also set up themes for their employees to think about ways to improve, such as "Lets have a war against waste."

10 Wastes

1. Unnecessary motion
2. Having excess inventory
3. Producing quality defects
4. Waiting time or delays, any storage—people or materials
5. Producing ahead or behind schedule, overproduction, not processing correctly
6. Set-up time
7. Inspection
8. Transportation or moving things
9. Excess costs, excess overhead
10. Not encouraging people to be creative, underutilizing people's talents and knowledge

Waste is any activity that does not add value to the product. Adding value is when you convert raw materials into finished goods, like bending metal, painting, cutting, polishing, extruding plastic, etc. When you take raw materials such as steel and rubber and convert them into a finished automobile, that is adding value. It is what manufacturing is all about.

The Idea Generator – Quick and Easy Kaizen

When you add your knowledge to marketing and selling a product, telling people how to better utilize your product or service, you are adding value.

When you improve your service to your customers and more and more customers are satisfied with your service you are adding value.

But when you begin to measure the value-adding time versus the non-value-adding time, you discover that in most companies 95% of the time is devoted to waste. The secret of modern manufacturing and the service industry today is to reduce or totally eliminate the non-value adding wastes. When you implement a Kaizen you are adding value.

Many of the items listed above are necessary to the production process and also to the service industry, and some cannot be entirely eliminated. But surely they can be reduced. Inspection is important to ensure that products are produced correctly, but it does not add value to the product. It is better to produce perfect products without inspection.

Call centers spend a lot of time monitoring employees speaking with customers. It might be better to not monitor and sample customers to see if they are pleased with the service.

Set up themes to challenge and inspire people to help your company succeed. Ask them to come up with ideas to reduce cost and wasted time. Ask them to discover better ways to please your customers. You can always find things to improve, always. You can help to excite people by coming up with a new theme each month. For example you might like to focus on improving safety this month.

In searching for improvement themes, you might like to add to your list the Japanese four K's and the five S's.

Four K's
1. Kusai – things that smell bad
2. Kitsui – things that are hard or dark
3. Kitanai – things that are dirty
4. Kiken – things that are dangerous

Just ask team members to go on a treasure hunt to find things on this list and recommend ways to improve.

Five S's
1. Seiri – sort things out, keep only needed items
2. Seiton – put things in order, organize them, ready to use
3. Seiso – keep things neat and clean,
4. Seiketsu – clean after use, everything in running order
5. Shitsuke – discipline, follow standards

Five S practices can be very effective in eliminating problems before they occur. And they are excellent concepts to use to inspire people's improvement ideas.

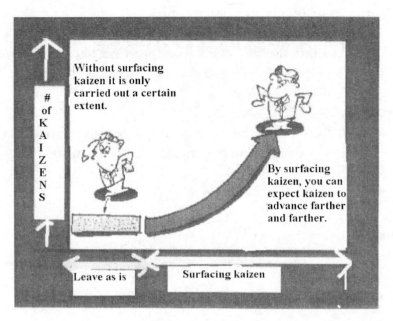

If you look, you can always find things to improve!

Transportation is necessary at times, but within a factory it can usually be reduced drastically. I remember seeing a video produced by Mercury Marine a manufacturer of outboard motors. They followed a part being manufactured throughout the production process. It originally traveled 26 miles back and forth in the plant. After they learned the Just-In-Time method and focused on reducing wastes, that part only traveled 100 feet while it was being manufactured.

3 Obstacles or Blocks to a creative idea system:

1. Attitude that the average employee is happy to just do their job everyday and to not think about change or improving their work.

2. Attitude that the average employee just doesn't have any good ideas on how to make improvements.

3. You don't ask – you don't get.

Summary

1. Do not question the source of the idea. Apply good methods, more and more. Welcome imitation.

2. Stop, reduce, change, imitate, and copy. Don't be locked into the wrong way of doing things.

3. Look, Listen, Study, and Copy what other companies are doing.

4. To implement Kaizen, practice Kaizen activities continuously. Do not simply do Kaizen and leave it there, you must also write it down and share it with other people.

5. A task today is to write down one Kaizen you have already done in your workplace, in a concise manner, using the Kaizen form below.

Chapter 14: Concluding Remarks

"Don't fear failure so much that you refuse to try new things. The saddest summary of a life contains three descriptions: could have, might have, and should have."

Louis Boone

Key Points of this book

1. **What is Kaizen: Our 3 Definitions of Kaizen.**

   a. Shortcut by changing methods. To accomplish your job objectives better, you select the means and methods. You get results through ingenuity rather than labor. Everybody can do it and understand.

   b. Small changes rather than big changes. You change the way you do your work little by little. Since they are small changes, they can be done quickly and easily. However, just a one-time small change is no good. The important thing is to continue.

   c. Changes within realistic constraints, within the limited conditions. Find what we can do and find a method we can do. We start with those things we can do for now and then save those we cannot do for later.

2. 3 Rules of Kaizen.

a. Stop doing unnecessary things. Don't stick to the way it has always been done.

b. Reduce. If you cannot stop doing unnecessary things, try to reduce them somehow.

c. Change. There are several methods to accomplish the same objectives. Change the factors or substitute and so forth.

3. 3 basic Principles of Kaizen.

a. Attack part by part. Divide the problem and start with a small part.

b. Attack from a different angle.

c. Attack at a different level. Start with what you can do right now.

LPIP
Learn – Practice – Improve - Perfect

"WHAT SETS US APART?
The Toyota Production System is at the heart of
everything we do. Based on the concept of continuous
improvement, or kaizen, every Toyota team member is
empowered with the ability to improve their work
environment. This includes everything from quality and
safety to the environment and productivity. Improvements
and suggestions by team members are the cornerstone of
Toyota's success."

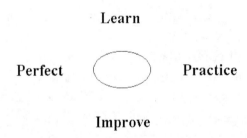

We all know the importance of treating our customers well. But very few of us spend the time to <u>Learn</u> the fundamentals of good service, to <u>Practice</u> those fundamentals every single day, to find ways to <u>Improve</u> our techniques, to internalize them, and <u>Perfect</u> them, and make them our own standard of excellence.

In all my trips to Japan I watched how the Japanese have so carefully studied almost every aspect of America. After World War II, their cities and industries were almost totally destroyed. They were devastated and their society looked so primitive in comparison with America; we were involved in the war but our cities were never bombed. Their goal was to begin again, to start something new instead of just re-building and replicating what was destroyed. They took their cameras, scraped up whatever limited money they had, and came to America to study us and to learn from us, the leaders of the industrial world. They would visit our factories, tell us how wonderful we were, and asked to take our pictures. Then they went back and copied us 100%. They saw how we did it and tried to reproduce our manufacturing methods exactly. They admired America and appreciated our help.

I worked once with the Japan Management Associations in Tokyo. After World War II, they came to the United States and visited the offices of the American Management Associations and went back to copy virtually exactly what they had seen. The classroom sizes were identical. The blackboards and even the chair sizes and shapes were identical. Like a child who learns by copying his parent, the Japanese admired us and copied us in almost every detail.

Yes, they <u>Learned</u> very well. Then they <u>Practiced</u> what they had learned to produce their own products and services. They practiced over and over again until they got it right. And then they <u>Improved</u> on what they had learned and practiced. And they <u>Perfected</u> or standardized it to obtain consistently high quality products and services.

I remember on the first study mission back in 1981, that most Americans looked at Japan only as a nation of copiers. But, we were wrong. Oh, yes they did copy us, but then they greatly improved on what they had seen. In 1960, we laughed at things made in Japan; we considered it to be "junk." In fact, Toyota had to recall the first cars shipped to America and take them back to Japan. But look at Toyota today!

Japanese industry <u>Learned, Practiced, Improved</u> and then <u>Perfected</u> their style. They started to produce some of the highest quality products in the world. And they encouraged their entire workforce to be more creative through the Kaizen system.

We have not held back. Everything is here in this book to help you install and sustain a Quick and Easy Kaizen system. We feel that implementing employee's creative ideas, empowering them to make decisions that affect their work and their relationship with their customers, is truly the only way for them to be involved. Coming to work every day and doing what they are told is not what we mean by involvement. Being a part of your company's creative process is involvement, being empowered to make decisions, working with team activities, fully participating is the best way to help people grow.

Now that you have learned the principles of Quick and Easy Kaizen, it is up to you and your staff to practice it every day. Through practicing Quick and Easy Kaizen you will learn the real power of this and probably you will say, "Why didn't we do this before?"

As you practice and find the best way of doing things, then you should perfect it, or standardize it, so that you get predictable and successful results.

Summary

Dream the kind of world you would like to live in and then make that world your very own.

In the age of craftsmen, over a century ago, the carpenter, the tinsmith, and other artisans were all highly skilled professionals. Young people started in life as beginners and apprentices, and they studied and worked many years for a master, learning the skills of their trade. These crafts people were skilled in all phases of their trade, from knowing the needs and desires of their clients to the exact products to build and deliver. To build a chair, for example, the carpenter knew the size of the client, their tastes for comfort, design, and use. The carpenter then selected the wood and then cured, cut, shaped, glued, sanded, polished, varnished, and delivered the finished chair to the client. The carpenter was involved in all aspects of the total manufacturing process.

Then came the age of work simplification, work specialization, and the industrial age. Henry Ford, Frederick Taylor, and others simplified work to improve productivity. Ford was able to reduce the cost of an automobile, double the pay of his workers, and also develop the richest company in the world. Other companies quickly followed, and for the next hundred years wealth poured into America. But the worker, who as a craftsperson had an enormous sense of pride in his job, now came to work each day to do a simple repetitive task. During this period, workers were very rarely asked for their ideas on how to improve their jobs, even though they knew their jobs better than anyone else. They did what was asked of them. They earned their money at work and had to find self-satisfaction elsewhere.

But now we are in a new millennium, the information age, with the power of the Internet becoming available to people and industries around the world. American society is swiftly going forward, but now is the time to rethink the very nature of work and reexamine and reapply the best from our past. The worker in this new age will once again be highly skilled. It is the only way we will be able to compete internationally.

Carpenters primarily competed with each other in the same village, but today's companies must compete with those in every country in the world. China and India, with a billion people each, are fiercely growing. At the same time they are developing, educating and building new skills to match our own. They can also use the Internet and the latest technologies, while paying their workers one-thirtieth of what the average American makes. A vast change is coming, quite possibly even greater than the industrial revolution.

To meet this challenge, we must eliminate all wastes. And the greatest waste is not harnessing the creative ability of every single employee. That's exactly why Quick and Easy Kaizen can have an effective place in this new age. Everyone is truly an expert. But those experts, your employees, must study to improve, must build up new skills, and must fully participate in the improvement process. And the fastest way to help people grow is to give them a new mechanism to inspire their personal development. Quick and Easy Kaizen is that tool. You start off very simply, getting people involved by submitting small change ideas, on a continuous basis, changes that can make their work easier and more enjoyable. You start off very easy, supporting and encouraging the workers to make frequent improvements. You also start a process to teach them new skills.

It says in the bible that, "God created man in his own image." No matter what your religion or belief I am sure you recognize that hidden inside each person is a vast potential often untapped. It is management's job to bring out the creativity from every employee in the company. What worked in the industrial age of the last century, where people did only repetitive tasks, will surely not work to our advantage today.

Quick and Easy Kaizen is a simple but powerful mechanism to stimulate everyone to come up with small improvement ideas. It is vitally important to the individual worker and, collectively, it can give your company a significant difference in the marketplace.

> *The best way to get a good*
> *idea is to get lots of ideas.*
> **Linus Pauling**

Gary Corrigan, VP Corporate Communications at Dana Corporation, was recently quoted in The New York times as saying, "In down times, having an idea program will make the difference. It creates a competitive advantage." We believe and know this is true.

We thank you for reading our book and hope you will continue reading the interviews we have printed in Part IV. We hope you will apply the ideas here to your own work environment, and we wish you great success. We would also love to hear about your successes. E-mail us at bodek@pcspress.com.

Part IV

Interviews with:

Jack Simms

Pat Pilleri

Dan Cavanagh

John Leech

Part IV Overview

We have now presented to you a methodology to get you started with a powerful participative program: The Idea Generator - Quick and Easy Kaizen. It works! It works very well! At this time, we suggest you gather a group of managers and employees together, and review the rules, principles and definitions of Kaizen. Then ask every employee in the company to think about ideas that they have implemented in the last year, and to write down two of those ideas on a simple Quick and Easy Kaizen memo form. Post those ideas onto a bulletin board or a wall, where everyone can see, and ask people in small groups to talk about those ideas.

Ask all employees to continue to focus on:

1. Improving customer service
2. Improving the quality of the products, or the services
3. Reducing costs
4. Improving safety
5. Reducing the time that it takes to serve customers or produce products

Then ask all employees to continue to come up with two improvement ideas each month. At Dana Corporation every manager including the chairman of the board submits ideas each month.

You might also ask all of your managers and many of your employees to read this book a chapter at a time, and then meet in small groups to discuss how to apply the concept in your company.

The Idea Generator – Quick and Easy Kaizen

Or you might conduct or ask us to conduct an in-house workshop. We've found the workshops to be a catalyst to help you get started.

Once you start the process, just following the rules and principles will allow you to continue successfully. Soon your company will begin to have its own brand of Quick and Easy Kaizen.

In the following Part IV, we have included four interviews with Dana Corporation managers. Jack Simms is the Idea Coordinator at a Dana plant in Statesville, North Carolina. Jack Simms has a system installed almost identical to the one explained in our book. It is system that focuses on implemented ideas.

Pat Pilleri, John Cavanaugh, and John Leech work at three different Dana locations. Each has an Idea system that works very powerfully and works very well, but their systems require very strong leadership abilities and experience managing an idea system.

We have included these interviews to show you where you might proceed to after you have installed and practiced Quick and Easy Kaizen for a few years. Their Idea systems are based on implemented ideas, but they also allow employees to fully communicate ideas that might have to be installed by others. These systems even allow people to send any kind of memo directly to the plant manager, including complaints. Their system requires unusual dedication. Each and every workday, the manager gathers all ideas submitted by employees. He or she reads them, then delegates many of the ideas to immediate subordinates, and every employee's idea is responded to within 24 hours. Pat Pilleri, plant manager at Hopkinsville, Kentucky told me that he spends at least 50 percent of his time each day working on those ideas. He has recognized the power that is unleashed when his employees fully participate in submitting and installing their ideas.

Start with Quick and Easy Kaizen, and make it work. Then, after a few years, consider proceeding with caution to the next level, as these managers have. We wish you the best in your journey to world class excellence.

"Do Not Block the Way of Inquiry"
- Charles S. Pierce

"...you can't eat a big fish all in one bite.
You've got to eat it one bite at a time.
I want these teams to realize that it's
lots and lots of small ideas that we really need."
Jack Simms

The following is an interview with Jack Simms, Ideas Coordinator with the Dana Corporation, first published in the Perfect Customer Service newsletter. Dana's system at this plant in Statesville, North Carolina operates very closely to the fundamentals of Quick and Easy Kaizen, with the objective of getting maximum participation from all employees. A system that gathers ideas from all employees can be your most effective tool to improve internal communications, to improve the quality of your products, to reduce waste, to improve customer service, and also to improve employee satisfaction. You can tell your associates what to do, but I believe you can be much more successful if you ask them their opinions, and gather their ideas on how to improve. Then you listen to those ideas and give them the tools and techniques to implement those ideas. You are then empowering them. Jack Simms is a great believer that the employee in his/her 25 square feet of space is the expert in their area. And if you want to make real accomplishments then you go and ask the expert.

BODEK: To begin, can you tell me a little bit about yourself and what you do at the plant?

SIMMS: I have been with the plant in Statesville [since] before it was Dana. I was part of the acquisition in 1997. I started in 1996—came in as a machinist. One of my first responsibilities was to sweep and mop floors. What I did didn't matter as long as they weren't telling me to do something illegal or immoral or harmful to my health. In about three weeks I went from sweeping and cleaning to running a roll spline machine for rolling axle shafts, which required about six weeks of training. On my very first day in the plant in September 1996, at 9:00 o'clock in the morning, there was a meeting in the front parking lot to announce that Ingersoll-Rand was going to sell the facility. Dana purchased the Statesville operation in February 1997. I was involved in rolling axle shafts for about a year and a half when the opportunity came up to bid on the Ideas Coordinator's job. I bid on that job in March 1998, and got the job and still have it. But the job has expanded somewhat. I serve as the Ideas Team Coordinator on the staff of Steve Moore, who is the plant manager. I was given the opportunity last year for Excellence In Manufacturing (EIM) training. That was a seven-month course. At the end of the course I was certified to train in team building.

BODEK: *Where did you take the course?*

SIMMS: It was in seven different Dana facilities, one week each month for seven months. It was an "Educate the Educator" EIM course. That was a fantastic experience for me. We were 15 people from varied backgrounds, not really understanding what the EIM process is all about. But each month we saw a little more light at the end of the tunnel and it became very clear that this was not just something to be doing for a day, but it was going to be an ongoing process. It's not something that we do once or twice a week. It is a way of life. And when we follow the process every day then we know we can continuously improve.

312

EIM needs everybody's ideas. As Ideas Coordinator, I'm very supportive. It's not my program. It's the people of Statesville's ideas program. I just happen to be the cheerleader, the 'exciter.' To ride; watch over it. To encourage, to report, to share and to help wherever I can. If it were my program then it probably would be a very dull program. Because it's not, it's a very exciting program. That's why I get really intense if I hear someone refer to it as a 'suggestion' program.

We describe in our handbook the value of the small, self-implemented ideas versus a suggestion. A suggestion is a statement you would submit for someone to do this or that. You're not taking ownership when it's a suggestion. But when it's an idea, you involve yourself in it and you do this, this, and this to achieve that. So, we've got to use that independent behavior, and this is where the team building comes in. We have to take that independent behavior and build it into interdependent to be successful. So the ideas program and team building really go hand in hand. They complement each other very well.

BODEK: *Do you get any team building training yourself?*

SIMMS: Yes. The seven-month EIM training was definitely the launching pad for team building. I had a lot of experience before coming here. I was Operations Manager for Pepsi-Cola for ten years. I was Director of Operations for Coca-Cola for four. One focal point of EIM is that a team is better than the strongest individual. Regardless of how good you are, if you and I work together then you're going to be better and I'm going to be better.

BODEK: *Explain EIM. Define it for me.*

SIMMS: I've got two definitions. One is the real one and one is kind of silly. EIM is Excellence In Manufacturing, the whole process of manufacturing. You can be excellent in all aspects. Or you can just get by. In the technical side of Dana University, they teach and train EIM.

When I started the seven-month course of Educate the Educator, I was my normal weight. When I finished I had gained 28 pounds.

BODEK: *Please also give us the silly one.*

SIMMS: So my silly definition is that EIM means 'Eating In Motion.' While attending the seven-month course of Educate the Educator, I would intensely study during the day and each evening, along with the other students, eat gobbles of ice cream. I gained 28 pounds in seven months.

When you have a facility that has some age on it you get stuck in a paradigm. Because you've done something a certain way doesn't mean it's the wrong way, but it doesn't mean it's the only way. There is a saying we use, and I am sure you've heard it: If you continue to do what you have always done, you continue to get what you always got.

We know that we are being thrust into a world market. We do not only compete with companies here in the United States; we have got a global market that we have to compete in and also provide goods to. So the way to do that is through the sharing of ideas. I am very strong in this statement that it's today's ideas that secure tomorrow's future.

The Idea Generator – Quick and Easy Kaizen

And then team involvement: If you have an idea and you are by yourself, you just have an idea. But if you have an idea and you and I are a team, and I have an idea, then we have two ideas.

BODEK: *Is this a full time role for you as Ideas Coordinator?*

SIMMS: Yes sir.

BODEK: *Tell me some of the things that you do in your role as coordinator.*

SIMMS: At least once a day I am on the shop floor going from work center to work center, especially the work centers where I am not seeing ideas being generated by a particular individual. I ask about what's going on. Some folks do not want to chitchat, but then some folks like to chitchat. We are involved in supporting our Dana Dodge Race Truck in a program called, "Whom do you pick?" And I happen to be the crew chief of that program as well. So that gives me a good opening to say, "Did you see the race this past weekend?" That gets our conversation going and I say, "By the way I have not noticed any ideas from you lately." I may get a response from him, "Well gee, Jack, I am filling them out and I give them to my manager." Then I would say something like, "Well let me check that for you."

BODEK: *What percentage of the people participates in this program?*

SIMMS: Our measurable goal is that we want two ideas per person per month. We want 80 percent implementation with 100 percent participation. For June we had 89 percent implementation but only 79 percent participation, which is not so stellar a month.

BODEK: *Tell us a little about how you handle the process when you receive an idea?*

SIMMS: We changed the structure on how ideas are reviewed. We changed to a manager-team concept. When I get the idea card I give the individual the credit. If it needs review, it goes right back to that manager and his team will sit down and review that idea. This way the idea card is not sitting on someone's desk.

And so what happens is the team can talk to the person who wrote it and say you know that's not a good idea. Why did you write that?

So the writer knows right then and there the status of his idea. But let's say that they decide that it's a great idea, but we need to invite somebody next week to our meeting from maintenance to help with the project. So now we get cross-functional sharing of ideas. They also might invite a person from maintenance.

BODEK: *Explain what you mean by Kaizen Blitz.*

SIMMS: Okay. An example of a Kaizen Blitz would be, let's say, you have an area of the plant that is not functioning properly. Maybe it's not laid out well. Let's say it was put together by a group of folks and the people on the shop floor were totally not a part of the decision. But yet they were told to make it work. The Dana style is to involve everybody in the facility to make something work. Our mission statement I think sums it up real well. "We promote the ongoing participation of Dana people in the continuous improvement of our products and processes to provide the highest level of service to our internal as well as our external customers." We acknowledge that we have the internal customers and, if we do not recognize that, then the plant and the company would be a very sad place to work. Because everybody's got a customer.

For the Kaizen Blitz we will share ideas; we will brainstorm to come up with ideas. Then the Kaizen Blitz is a period of time when we say okay, tomorrow at seven o'clock we are going to attack this portion of the facility and this is what we are going to do. We are not talking about it. We are going to do it. And we get together many members and make a cross functional team. We cannot take just the workers in that area. We got to get maintenance people, electricians. Then we got to bring somebody in from the outside to be a part of that Kaizen Blitz. And that is a very key point. We need that outsider asking the all-important questions.

BODEK: *Tell me about this Kaizen Blitz. Is this primarily getting ideas or are you reviewing the whole process flow and improving the flow?*

SIMMS: It's getting ideas to be able to execute the blitz. And the blitz is like I was explaining. Tomorrow morning at seven o'clock with these ideas we are going to change the way this line is laid out.

I mean it's improvement time now. Everybody on that team wears a red shirt. Okay? It might take us 12 hours to do it, or eight hours, but we stay with it until that blitz is completed. Then we have a report session with the staff. We tell them what we did, and here's the result. And this is what we are going to do three months from now. We are going to come back and blitz it again, and we are going to tweak it and make it better. So it's a continuous improvement process.

BODEK: *How many people normally participate in a blitz?*

SIMMS: It depends on the area. I have been involved in them where I have had as few as four people and as many as 16. But 15 is getting to be a stretch.

When you start getting that many people, it just starts getting out of hand. Then people come and they just sit around and they are not really participating. When I took the Educate the Educator course, I wanted to know how DANA wanted to conduct a Kaizen Blitz. Not a Kizan, a Kaizen. There is a difference. Kizan is what most Americans say, and when they are around Japanese if they say Kizan the Japanese start kind of laughing under their breath because Kizan means to cover up. Kaizen means to improve. So you have to be careful when you say Kaizen.

BODEK: *Kaizen does mean continuous improvement, like the old barber's pole, which showed the colors continuously spiraling upward. Continuous improvement continues, one idea builds on top of another, and never stops.*

SIMMS: A principle of Kaizen is that you will attack a problem and then come back and revisit it. And you will attack it again until it cannot be improved any more. Another thing with the ideas program is that I want to make sure people are encouraged to write their ideas down.

People say, "But Jack, that is my job." Okay, great. How many times have you come up with an idea, shared it with your supervisor, and have him slough it off saying it's not a very good idea; go on back to work. Then a month later you see your idea being implemented, and somebody else is getting the bows and all the accolades.

BODEK: *Right. It happens so often.*

SIMMS: It happens all the time. When I was 12 years old I was part of a writing class and we were charged with writing a commercial. I came up with this brilliant commercial idea for BIC pens. A father and son are out in the woods on an overnight camp out, and the little boy says, "Daddy, we forgot a can opener to open the beans." But dad's got a BIC pen in his front pocket. He says, "Don't worry, son," and with the BIC pen he starts punching holes in the can to open it. Then the little boy says, "But daddy, you'll ruin the pen." He says, "Son, this is a BIC. It writes the first time, every time." My teacher thought it was a fantastic ad. We sent it off to BIC. Several weeks later we got a letter back saying thank you for your interest but that is was not a commercial idea, we could not use it, but eight months later we saw that commercial aired on TV.

It was not a can of beans. It was a soft drink can.

Well, one premise of the Ideas Program is that we do not only say it but we have to believe it, and we have to make people believe that they are the experts in their 25 square foot areas.

When I first heard that, I thought it was a really hokey statement, that you are the expert in your 25 square foot area. I just finished a team-training course two weeks ago. It was a five-day class, and 98 people went through the class here in Statesville—all of Statesville's managers and leadership people. When we really open our eyes and really believe that we are the experts in our 25 square foot areas, we realize that Steve Moore, plant manager, doesn't want to run everything in the plant. He doesn't know how to run a CNC lathe. He doesn't know how to run a welder. He doesn't know how to run a roll-splicing machine. But, he knows the plant processes. He knows production scheduling and costs. Then it's his job to give the tools to the operators and they become the experts in their 25 square foot areas.

I know you have seen Joel Barker's video, "The Business of Paradigms." It's a very powerful video. It shows that it's the new guy that has got the new ideas. In church, a couple of Sundays ago, the story was told about David. Why was he so different from everyone else in the whole army of Israel? He did not have a military paradigm. He did not know he could not go out and kill that giant. He had the faith that God told him he could do it. He did not know that he needed a big sword or a big shield or a big helmet. All he needed was what God told him he needed and he had the faith and the hope that he was going to use his sling and a stone and kill the giant.

BODEK: *Yes.*

SIMMS: If he had been bogged down with the military paradigm he never would have killed that giant.

I guess the key to my job is that I've got to be infectious. I keep trying every day and I know that it's almost an impossibility to please everybody. I'm not going to be able to please everybody. But I do not stop and I do not give up trying to do that. Because of my chemistry and my make up, if I know that somebody's got an ax to grind about me or the Ideas Program that I'm responsible for, then I go to confront them.

BODEK: *What kinds of awards are there for people?*

SIMMS: There are no rewards for ideas.

The Idea Generator – Quick and Easy Kaizen

Now, I receive every idea. Our idea cards are blue, three by five cards printed with the worker's name, department number, and shift. They write the idea and check if the idea is implemented, or needs review, and then we have a row of boxes at the bottom to check. Does the idea deal with safety? Quality? Throughput? Customer satisfaction? Customer service? Cost savings? The idea has to deal with one of those categories.

Let's say you and I work next to one another. You come up with an idea that improves what you are doing. I'm over there. I'm struggling. I walk over to the board. I look at that idea to see what you have done. Wow, you did that? Well then I could submit the same idea. It doesn't matter if it's your idea. If I can do the same thing in my work area, it's another improvement. Why reinvent the wheel? They have implemented that idea in their work area to reduce cost, to improve set-up, to do something that is tangibly to the benefit of the company. But they can't just write the idea and not implement it.

I mean these are ideas like this one. I've got it right in front of me. One individual is responsible for spindle drives, and when they have been needing repair he has been shipping them out, which takes three weeks. He came up with the idea that he can replace parts in the spindle drive, saving $2,400 and only taking two days to repair it and put it back into operation. That is a cost-saving idea.

So now we get cross-functional sharing of ideas. They invite a person from maintenance, and they become a team. I just had the list here in front of me. We've got 72 active teams working in the Statesville facility.

BODEK: *Now on these teams, what do you do in the office environment? Do they have teams too?*

SIMMS: Oh sure. There might be somebody from the accounting department on a shop floor team.

BODEK: *But they might have their own team in the office?*

SIMMS: Yes. Then they'll have accounting issues that they will be working on.

And why are we doing that? Because the concept got ingrained here in Statesville that it was the million-dollar idea that really counted. But see, you can't eat a big fish all in one bite. You've got to eat it one bite at a time. I want these teams to realize that it's lots and lots of small ideas that we really need.

People in the office areas are as much involved as plant people. They are expected to turn in their ideas, too. The political environment here is really unique. The plant manager, Steve Moore, turns in three or four more ideas than anybody else in the plant. He leads by example. If you are a staff person you better not have me come up at the end of a month and say I didn't get any ideas from you.

I couldn't do what I do if I didn't believe in what I am doing. I give 180% in what I teach and I couldn't do that if I didn't believe in what I'm doing.

The team training here is to me just really unique because it deals with things in the plant that people can relate to. There are exercises that we do away from the plant that really demonstrate that a team is better than the strongest individual. I came up with a three-day bowling exercise that is just phenomenal. In the middle of a class all of a sudden I say, "Everybody stand up. Get your stuff. We are going to go bowling." They think, "Man this is crazy." But we bowl for three days in a row, but every day we change the situation. We change the structure. They have no idea what is going on until the third day, and the next day we have hours of discussion on what we went through. It is just phenomenal.

BODEK: *Jack thanks an awful lot. I'll be in touch with you again.*

Please Take Greatness
from Wherever it Comes

"...anybody can say anything they want
without getting in trouble. Once you've
gained that kind of respect from people
then you got yourself a great operation."
Pat Pilleri

This interview with Pat Pilleri, Plant Manager with Dana Corporation, discusses another variation of Kaizen. While the main focus of Quick and Easy Kaizen is to encourage people to implement small ideas to improve their own work, this Dana system, at this particular plant, allows an interesting approach to the idea improvement process. Imagine finding a way whereby your employees become your teachers, and also finding a technique

*where open trust and full and honest communication exists. This is
a rare find but I hope that it will be replicated throughout America.*

BODEK: *Jack Simms let the cat out of the bag and told me about
your most unusual but very effective management style. You manage a manufacturing plant with around 750 people, and 114 of
them are trainers?*

PILLERI: That is correct.

BODEK: *It sounds very intriguing. Please tell me first a little bit
about yourself and what you do in the plant, what the plant does,
and then maybe we can talk about your idea system, and especially
who your 114 trainers are and what they do.*

PILLERI: Well, first, I am just a plant manager. I just try to make
sure everything stays on an even keel, and sometimes in a 750-
person plant that could be somewhat difficult, but really my only
job I have is to manage, just to manage a plant and all aspects of it.
That is my job in a nutshell.

Also part of that function of managing is listening to people.
Listening to people: it is very, very important. I can sit here all
day long and make all the rules I want, when I am talking to people, and that is truly a mistake. I tend to let people know during
meetings if a particular change is going to come up in one of our
policies. If I think a particular change has to be made, or to review
our quality policy, or to ramp up our new production, I first talk
about it at plant meetings and then I talk to people about it after-
wards, and I do not have to seek the conversation. The people
come to seek me out and they tell me what they think of each idea
or each change that is going to be made or each new system, or

anything like that, plus they feed me a whole lot of information through the idea system. So I am managing a plant and, I guess, listening to people is a big, big part of managing a plant. That is what I do. I spend—I've got to believe 50% of my time talking to people.

That has really, really helped. It's helped the entire operation.

Now as far as the number of trainers, when we have a program or somebody feels, anybody in the plant, any plant floor person, or anybody in the plant … has an idea about where they feel we would need more training. And that could be with a process, with a particular piece of machinery, with the whole assembly line, with anything at all in the plant. Once a person comes up with that idea, we then ask that person to put together the training materials for that particular task that is going to be improved. It may be, for example, an improved safety program. It may be an improved productivity program. It may be an improvement with one of our processes. It may be an improvement with a piece of equipment. It may be an improvement with a particular machine. It may be an improvement in how we fix things, but no matter what, once a person comes forward with that idea we ask them to put the actual training materials together themselves. We ask them to outline actually for us what exactly is it that you think we should be teaching in this particular class. Then once we look it over, of course, then once approved, we let the person who came up with the idea, we let them do the teaching themselves.

That is why we have 114 trainers on various subjects, and they do it, honest to God, Norman, they do it with a whole lot of enthusiasm, and much, much more enthusiasm than you and I could ever have in teaching a class like this because it was their idea to begin with. We call that our People Training People program. It has been very, very successful for us. We use our plant employees also to train new hires. They are very, very good at it. They are extremely good at it. After every class I ask for comments about the trainers themselves, ask for comments and what people thought of the class and it's just unbelievable the comments that are made, but are actually documented, of what people think of the trainers, and how well it was conducted, and how well the class was conducted, and so forth and so on. So we have really, really proven that to be worthwhile for us.

You wanted to know about was our idea system. Well, we believe in keeping things simple, and there is in fact no such thing as a suggestion form. Some plants utilize a form, usually an 8-1/2 x 11 form asking them for a whole lot of different information. Other plants, they don't accept just an idea. But you know, you have to understand, I am not saying those things are wrong, what I am saying is that in our particular plant and every plant has a different personality but here we keep it simple. Keep it as simple as possible. I know of several plants that won't accept an idea unless you implement it yourself, which is both good and bad I think, you know, unless you implement the idea yourself. Things like that there.

We're very, very flexible. All a person does is use a 3" x 5" yellow card to write his idea on. And what he does with that card is he sticks it up, and we refer to it as a "Story Board." A storyboard, if you will, just use thumbtacks and it is kind of like a bulletin board and they just stick it up there with a thumbtack and then somebody else will come along and we will have a spin-off of that idea. They will put up their 3" x 5" inch yellow card on that board and so forth and so on. If there's a particular problem any place in the plant, a person might see it, and submit an idea. It could be an opinion, a statement, a complaint, I don't care, but [there's] one thing I do care about and that is communication.

So, really, what we have in place is really truly a communications system, rather than a real technically true idea system. It's really a communications system. It's a way for people to communicate, not only with me and my plant staff and their supervisors, but also to communicate with everybody else and it works very, very effectively. The ideas are just unbelievable. The imaginations that our people have is just great. I mean just absolutely fantastic.

Ideas posted here daily.

I collect, personally, all of the yellow cards, everyday, on the two boards. And the rule is that nobody takes a yellow card down from the board except Pat and that's it. Now, this board I am talking about, the storyboard, or bulletin board, there's also a lock box.

The lock box

We have two of them in the plant. This lock box, if somebody wants to keep something private or confidential, they will take the yellow card and put it into that lock box and everybody in our plant knows that I am the only one in the whole plant with a key to this box. So for confidentiality, the purpose of confidentiality, sometimes people will get a little embarrassed maybe about putting up an idea or suggestion or something may not seem like it's really truly a good idea, but they've thought of it and those things will come up and they'll say "Pat, I'm really not sure about this idea of mine, I don't want people making fun of me if it's a bad idea so just please only you read it". Then I collect all the yellow cards and then I have a system whereby each and every yellow card gets an answer within 24-hours.

That also sends a strong, strong message that we listen to people, that, you know, we consider everybody's thoughts, opinions, statements, very, very valuable, and very, very valuable to the entire operation. So that's really our idea system in a nutshell. We have achieved 38 ideas per person this year, and that's a lot of ideas per person.

BODEK: *Wow. And YOU read every one of them?*

The Idea Generator – Quick and Easy Kaizen

PILLERI: Yes I do.

BODEK: *You are a very dedicated person reading on the average of 100 improvement ideas per day moving them throughout the plant so quickly. It is an amazing feat. What do you think is the percentage of those that you're able to install?*

PILLERI: The last time I looked at that number it was something like 82% implemented.

BODEK: *Of the 38 ideas submitted by a person with 82% of those installed, what percentage of the people that come up with the idea are able to install their own idea?*

PILLERI: I'd say a third, because sometimes people have got a really good idea about a piece of equipment. Now, not everybody possesses how to change a piece of equipment or a process. And not everybody has the same level of mechanical skills, electrical skills, electronic skills, and that kind of thing. So really if I said a third I don't think I'd be too far off.

BODEK: *A third. Okay now. Many different ideas just keep popping into my head. One is how do your supervisors handle people bypassing the normal channels, being able to deal directly with you?*

PILLERI: Well, this is the Dana Corporation, and in the Dana Corporation anybody can talk to anybody. Anybody can talk to anybody. There are no closed doors anyplace. I've had people go to corporate headquarters and stop in and chat with the chairman of the board just over nothing. You go over just say hello. I've had people do that on several occasions. I mean the chairman of the board of a $12 billion or $13 billion company. He welcomes people. He is very, very friendly with people.

So, you know, my answer is, I guess, clean and simple. This is the Dana Corporation and in the Dana Corporation anybody can talk to anybody and nobody takes it like you're going over my head and none of that stuff. Anybody can talk to anybody. I have my boss in here and he goes off on his own and talks to people and I've had the President of our Strategic Business Unit come in and he goes off and he talks with people on his own. The rule is that anybody can say anything. I mean really, and I'll tell you what, it works and people know that, and it gets people a feeling of confidence, that anybody can say anything they want without getting in trouble. Once you've gained that kind of respect from people then you got yourself a great operation.

BODEK: *You get an idea and you assign it to a person that you think they can handle it.*

PILLERI: That's absolutely correct. I assign it to the person that I think can handle it.

BODEK: *They accept that idea even though it didn't come from them.*

PILLERI: Oh my God, yes. We are very, very proud of the fact that everybody is given a response within 24-hours. Now, if it's a major project and a major job, of course, it doesn't have to be done in 24-hours. We can put it on our work list, if you will, our maintenance list of things to do. But it's very important that we tell the person that submitted it we think this is a great idea and we're going to do it and it'll be put into our work log immediately.

The Idea Generator – Quick and Easy Kaizen

And if it's not such a good idea it'll be explained to people that we don't particularly feel that this is the right thing to do because of this and that, and actually give reasons. We don't say just yes or no, we give reasons for not doing it. **There is no such thing as a bad idea.** No such thing. So, all in all, it's been a very, very successful program and it's helped us to become a successful operation. And that's not bragging, that's a fact.

BODEK: *Thank you for your time today, Pat.*

PILLERI: Norman, thank you, I enjoyed it. I guess you can tell.

I believe that Quick and Easy Kaizen is the way to start asking the "The Experts" in your company to become completely involved in change, in the improvement process. Maybe after you have succeeded with Quick and Easy Kaizen you might like to extend the process and adapt some of Pilleri's ideas. Probably both systems side-by-side would be better, Quick and Easy Kaizen for self-implemented ideas and the Pilleri system to improve communications in the company.

Ali Baba Shouted, "Open sesame!"

".... each person puts in three ideas every month, 36 ideas in a year; with 240 people in the plant that is 8640 ideas for improvement in one year. Think how powerful that is!"

Dan Cavanagh

You must learn to ask, to even shout, "How do we improve customer service?" And then you listen.

The principles to deliver superior customer service are simple, probably summarized by just "treating people the way you would like to be treated." You treat everyone fairly, wisely, respectfully, carefully, and cheerfully, as guests in your own home. It sounds so simple, but is so rarely applied. Why not? This past year we have given this a lot of thought. I think the main obstacle is our management system—this top down structure. The CEO conveys a message and everyone else in the organization tries to understand and follow those edicts. Of course, we need capable leadership and proper direction, but instead of management coming up with all the answers, we must, we should ask the people that do the work to come up with the solutions either individually or in teams.

At the beginning of this book, I quote Jack Simms at Dana, "Ask your employees this question: 'If you owned this company, what would you do to improve it?'" Go ahead, ask your employees that simple but powerful question, or ask them "What would you do to improve customer service?" And then listen, and listen and see how you can empower them to implement their own ideas.

335

I'm happy to share another interview, this one with Dan Cavanagh, plant manager of Dana Corporation Structural Products facility in Stockton, California. Whether or not you work for manufacturing companies, you will see the idea system as applied at this Dana plant can work equally well in the office or for an airline or any other type of company.

BODEK: *Dan, thank you for this interview. Please introduce yourself.*

CAVANAGH: After I received an MBA from Illinois Benedictine College with an emphasis in organization development, Dana made me a plant manager in Canada—it was kind of trial by fire. I spent three years in Canada. We set out to build a very strong team and were very successful. We became a number one supplier to our number one customer. We also received several supplier awards, including the Key West 9000, Chrysler Pedestal, and the list goes on and on. That plant is very successful. Dana, as part of my career development, sent me to this Stockton facility.

BODEK: *Ten years ago I lead Dana managers on several study missions to Japan, and now I understand that Toyota managers are coming to visit your plant.*

CAVANAGH: Mr. Ishi, president of NUMMI, a joint venture between Toyota and GM, did visit our plant. He told us we were doing a lot of things better than they were. Toyota has helped us and guided us. I recently had my first trip to Japan and I saw how our whole line and our production process came to be, which is very interesting. It's probably the best in America at this moment, at least from my investigations.

BODEK: *Please tell us what is so unique about it.*

The Idea Generator – Quick and Easy Kaizen

CAVANAGH: All right. I'll explain the system we have for ideas. First of all, our goal is three ideas per person per month. We routinely get more than two. We set a target of three ideas per person per month with 85 percent implementation. It is a very simple process. We just use a green index card. We call them green cards and we have the three locations in the plant where you can either post a suggestion for others to add to and contribute to or drop them in a box for the plant manager. Once a day, I will go through each of those areas and pick up all the ideas. I read each one of them, one by one, and assign each one to a staff member. Then I give those cards to an assistant who puts each of them on a piece of paper and gives them to the staff members they're assigned to. Then that person will give an answer in writing back to the teammate. We set a goal of 24-hour response on those ideas.

When I got here, responses were weak. And sometimes it would be months and the teammates haven't heard back. So we set a goal of 24 hours' turn-around. We run about 80% percent on that 24-hour turn-around.

In addition to that, to capture more ideas I started an "Ideas Generated" form that is used in all meetings. If you are holding a team meeting, the Ideas Generated form is used to document the ideas from the meeting. We found that the Ideas Generated form is a tremendous help for people who don't take the time to write a green card or aren't really confident in themselves about expressing their ideas. They may think their idea is a stupid idea or something. But if they just get into a conversation in the meeting, their ideas are captured by the team leader and assigned within the team, which helps our self-implementation of the ideas by the teams. It adds a tremendous boost for us.

BODEK: *How often do those teams meet?*

CAVANAGH: Once a week for 30 minutes. The whole production line shuts down on Thursday at 9:30am, and they break into their teams. Each team has there own measurable. We don't give them any kind of script. If we have announcements, we will go team to team and just make our little five-minute speech, but we let them decide what is important to them. The teams also, in the plant meetings, stand up and report on their measurable. Using a power point presentation, they describe the things they are doing and what they have done to improve.

BODEK: *Give me an idea of a measurable.*

CAVANAGH: They measure number of defects. They measure the number of cross-training hours. They measure their housekeeping, their five S's [sorting things out, putting things in order, keeping things neat and clean, cleaning after use, and discipline to maintain standards]. They measure their safety, those types of things.

We just started that last year and so far the teams' measurable are pretty common, but we are encouraging them to measure what is important to them as a team. Some of the teams are stepping out a little bit in measuring different things that are important to them.

BODEK: *What are the awards that you offer?*

CAVANAGH: We really don't. The only thing is that at the end of the year, if you hit the goal of 36 ideas or three per month, we will give you 50 dollars in Dana bucks, paper money towards Dana identity items and things like that. So we don't pay for the ideas. From my standpoint, philosophically, I don't agree on paying for ideas because continuous improvement of our entire plant ensures our survival. I think if you start paying for ideas, as soon as you stop paying your ideas stop. So we don't do that.

BODEK: *What is curious to me is the way Japan has had idea programs for 20 years, and they are paying for ideas.*

CAVANAGH: When you said that I was kind of cringing a little bit. We try to keep our idea program real simple. I've been involved with other idea programs that had forms to fill out with expected cost savings to calculate. That's too much detail as far as I am concerned, although a shortcoming of our program is that we don't calculate the savings. At this point in the evolution of the program it's more teammate involvement and self-implementation as much as possible. I see ourselves possibly moving to expected savings, and maybe that could be moving us toward an award-type system. We could make it a gain share if we achieve real savings and bring the savings to the bottom line. Then we could share the result.

BODEK: *It seems that each plant at Dana is unique in their approach to the idea program.*

CAVANAGH: That's what makes Dana what it is really. We don't have any corporate policy rules. It is just a guideline. The Dana Style and Policies sheet is one side of one sheet of paper. That is all we have. I have total responsibility for the bottom line of this facility and we decide what is best for us on the Dana style. My attendance policy is something we made up. I may benchmark other Dana facilities and see how they are doing it. I may benchmark their gain share plans, but we decide what is right for us. I think that's what makes Dana strong, actually.

BODEK: *I don't know of any other company that invests in people the way Dana does, investing in their education.*

CAVANAGH: We believe that the person out there doing the job is the expert, because I certainly am not the expert. We need their ideas to tell us how to improve. I could stand out there all day and I would never get it, compared with what they do every single day.

BODEK: *What kind of training do people get in your plant?*

CAVANAGH: We hire into a six-month temp-to-hire program. They start out on the production floor in a non-welding environment. They are out there for about a month, maybe just a couple of weeks. They then are evaluated by their teammates on the floor as to whether they recommend them to go to weld training.

When they get to weld training, that is where I come in, and I give them a one-hour presentation on the Dana Corporation, who we are, and what we are all about. I encourage them as they are going through this process to interview us as much as we are interviewing them. I talk about what we have to offer and I talk about what we expect from them in terms of commitment. In that meeting I talk about the green card process and the power of ideas. I emphasize how each person puts in three ideas every month, 36 ideas in a year…with 240 people in the plant that is 8640 ideas for improvement in one year. Think how powerful that is! At that point we start to give them an idea of the culture and that we want them to participate. I tell them, "You're the expert out there and you know best how to do the job. And we want you to be a team player." The rest of their training has to do with being a team player. When they finish weld training, they are assigned into a production team. We also have team-building days where we go through and we evaluate their team skills. We are not looking for expert welders here. We are looking for people who work in a team. In their team meeting they are now getting exposed to the Ideas Generated form and the green card system, and so very early on we kind of wrap the idea program into our culture. That is why we had to make an improvement to a turn-around in 24 hours. Then our teammates would believe they were being heard and were being answered when they put in their ideas.

BODEK: *I think it's fantastic that you read 8500 ideas a year.*

CAVANAGH: It really is not that difficult, to tell you the truth. We are kind of evolving on this to get more sophisticated ideas. When you start an idea program, everyone wants to ask well what's an idea? Put a definition on it. My opinion is you don't need to spend any time in defining ideas. If a guy wants to move the wastebasket from one side to the other, then get it done. Let him self-implement it, or even move it for him, because then he'll say okay someone's listening to me. Let's move forward and the ideas just grow with more recognition and more ideas are implemented.

BODEK: *You train people to do welding. The more you can educate them in everything in the plant, the more and better ideas you will get.*

CAVANAGH: Yes. We teach them financials so that they understand how the money runs through this plant. You're right. We also train them about the Toyota Production System (TPS). They go through an eight-hour training on one-piece flow. They need to understand that this is different from maybe any job they have ever had. It is Just-in-Time. We don't have a warehouse of parts that we are pulling from. Your hours worked could be all over the map depending on what the customer does. We are tied to that, be prepared for that. They understand the Andon boards [sign boards alerting to schedule or potential problems], Kaizen [continuous improvement], and the multi-elements of the Toyota Production System.

We just launched a plant-wide project this year called Lower Cycle Time [time taken to produce products]. We basically lowered our cycle time from 90 to 74 seconds. To do that, instead of getting my process engineers and production managers in the room and figuring it out, we threw it right to the teams. We said okay you got to get your cycle time down to 74 seconds. It was amazing, the feedback we got. They did all their own time studies. They came up with what they thought would include moving some welds from one team to another, changing parts locations and things like that as a team. Then they developed the work construction sheets and the standardized work forms. They did all the combination tables. We just launched it last week. It is just unbelievable, this beautiful thing—and they did it.

BODEK: *Who is on a team?*

CAVANAGH: For the production team, the line is divided into four different sections. So if you are working at a certain fixture you may be a part of team one. Team one might be the front half of the line. Team two may be the middle of the line. There are normally 20 people on a team.

BODEK: *Do you have people in your office involved with the green cards?*

CAVANAGH: Yes. They turn in/offer their ideas. They've got the same goals as everybody else. They may turn in/give ideas based on something they have seen on the floor or in their own department.

BODEK: *So if they do accounting work they are going to try to come up with a better way to do that accounting? Do you have any idea what the highest number of ideas was submitted by one person last year?*

CAVANAGH: I know this year it is my HR manager. She has 273 and we are all chasing her.

BODEK: *I thank you very much for your time.*

Another Look at a Great Idea System

*"Moreover, they tend to believe that truly creative
individuals are few and far between. We believe
the opposite. We all have a creative side, and it
can flourish if you spawn a culture to encourage it,
one that embraces risks and wild ideas and tolerates
the occasional failure. We've seen it happen."*

**Tom Kelley with Jonathan Littman
authors of The Art of Innovation**

*In our continued study of the best Idea System in America, we
interviewed John Leech, currently the general manager, American
Electronics Components division, Dana Corporation. When we
interviewed John a few months ago, he was the manager of a Dana
plant in Owensboro, Kentucky. Dana Corporation is one of the
world's largest suppliers of components, modules, and complete
systems to global vehicle manufacturers and their related after-
markets. The company operates some 300 major facilities in 35
countries and employs more than 75,000 people. The company
reported sales of $12.3 billion in 2000.*

BODEK: *Thank you for this interview. Please tell us a little
about yourself.*

LEECH: I started with DANA 15 years ago. I'm a
mechanical engineer by background. I graduated from Ohio State
University, immediately started at DANA, and worked in
applications engineering as a manufacturing engineer and then a
quality manager. Then I moved into plant management. Before
coming to Owensboro I spent four years with DANA/Japan in

Tokyo. I was responsible in 1997 for the startup of the facility in Owensboro.

BODEK: *And what do you make in the facility and tell me about your Idea System?*

LEECH: We make pickup frames for the Toyota Tundra pickup truck, and we are just now starting production for the Sequoia sport utility vehicle made by Toyota. We have a single customer; it's Toyota Motor Manufacturing, in Princeton, Indiana. We deliver to them on a just-in-time basis. We send to the Toyota plant about 16 trucks a day, about eight trucks a shift, with 25 frames per truck. We produce frames to meet the exact needs in the exact sequence to be installed on the Toyota production line.

We do have a TIP system. TIP is a good idea. I got a tip for you: TIP stands for Team Member Idea Program.

BODEK: *Could you tell me a little bit about the process and how it works?*

LEECH: It's a pretty simple system. The TIP by definition itself is a thought, a suggestion, a comment, a complaint, or an idea. It can just be anything. We view the system as a communication tool and it doesn't have to be the great suggestion that wins all kinds of dollar savings or anything like that. It can be just anything. Some of the best tips that we get are the tips that say, "Hey I think that such and such a coordinator is doing a great job," and ideas like that are certainly welcome. The TIP program starts off with a team member who has a tip. We use a blue, a kind of baby blue 3 x 5 note card, and there is nothing on the suggestion that says it is the cost savings or anything. It's just a card. We'll accept a tip written on anything, a napkin or a scrap of paper, however it works. An employee, individually, or as part of a team will fill out a tip or an idea or whatever their suggestion is and they post them on a TIP board. Our TIP board is located in the cafeteria, and daily I personally take the tips down and I review them.

I then assign them to one of about six people that are my direct reports, the plant management staff. Once I assign them, I initial them, put the dates down and then I hand all those tips to the human resource technician who puts a number on each of the tips. Then the tips are photocopied on an 8 ½ x 11 sheet of paper, recorded in a log — how many were received, who's inputted them, and where they go. We do this for tracking purposes. The original tip goes into a file box. The copy of the tip then goes to a manager who was assigned the tip and has the responsibility to answer the tip, or to assign the tip to someone else or to distribute it to the team member that made up the TIP. There is also a box for confidential ideas or suggestions that come directly to me that I will answer directly back to the submitter of the TIP.

BODEK: *You do accept ideas that will go to somebody else to do?*

LEECH: Oh, yes. I think that people feel a greater sense of pride and ownership when they implement their own idea, but people themselves just can't implement a lot of tips on their own. And again, to us it is not just an idea system but really it is a communication tool. For example, we are expanding our plant and one of the tips that came through is, "I think when we do this expansion we should have a showcase area to display our products to guests." That's not something that the individual can implement them selves, but it certainly is a good idea as we move forward and try to plan.

BODEK: *Great. You have 325 people in the plant. Tell me about the participation rates?*

LEECH: Around 60% of the people participate each month. The person who submits the TIP, which averages around 1.2 ideas per person, implements around 52% of the ideas.

BODEK: *How about yourself?*

LEECH: I turn my tips in. I have to be honest, I learn a lot reading through the tips given to me which triggers and idea for me then I'll sort of copy those down and throw my card in.

BODEK: *Do you compile any of these into a notebook for people to glance through?*

LEECH: We don't. What we do is take the top 20 tips or so every month and give them to a "TIP team." The TIP team reviews those top 20 and then, based on safety, quality, efficiency, cost savings, housekeeping, and whether or not it was implemented, they select and rank the top ten tips. Then in the plant meeting I give recognition to those people that submitted the top ten tips. The top tip of the month gets a 25-dollar gift certificate.

Our view is that giving tips and ideas really is part of our job and our duty, and one of the things we require of our team members is to get better and improve to provide the long-term security of this plant. The benefit is that we've made our jobs easier and we have some buy-in.

Certainly putting the emphasis on the idea program is what's going to move it forward. We've analyzed our TIP system and we want to improve it. The numbers I'm giving you are not counting tips that come through from team activities and team meetings.

One big battle that we have right now is that we are a new plant. About 50% of our people have less than six months of service, so as we move forward we're really trying to indoctrinate people about giving tips is a good thing, and is a way to communicate but its a hard culture to break. **I don't know where people have worked before, but you can just tell that giving ideas was not wanted.**

BODEK: *Yes, we know that many places ask people to come to work and leave their brains outside.*

LEECH: Exactly.

BODEK: *And this is a wonderful way of telling people how much you really respect them. So you're saying that an idea is really anything, it could be very trivial?*

LEECH: The story I like to use is that one of the very first tips that we had was posted on the card with the word "scissors". We looked at that and we go, "Scissors? What is going on here? Something's not right, it says, 'scissors.' There was no name signed to it, nothing. We found out who wrote the tip and we said scissors? What do you mean by this? And he said, "Well, I needed a pair of scissors," he says, "I didn't know how to go about getting a pair of scissors". We looked at that one tip and we started to analyze it, we realized that in many ways that tip said a whole lot of things on the surface that seemed very trivial. This guy just wrote down scissors and he just wanted a pair of scissors, but then it came to us that why didn't our people know how to get office supplies? He didn't understand how to go about ordering office supplies. He didn't understand the process. Maybe our indoctrination period, or introductory period, needed to address how do you go about getting office supplies. Then we revamped part of our introduction period with some of our new team members and sort of opened things up. What I see that appeared to be trivial sometimes on the surface really are addressing more fundamental and underlying ideas. That's what I really like about the tip suggestion system. The whole idea of when you put them on the board even a little idea may spark three or four more ideas.

And pretty soon they're all over the place from that one idea that was up there.

BODEK: *Historically, suggestion systems boggled down over ideas submitted for other people to do something with my idea. However, you and other Dana managers have carefully evolved this system to gain overall acceptance from your employees.*

LEECH: I think overall there are no real negatives. I am really impressed, especially with this work force, with the quality of the TIP system. I've been in other facilities where the TIP or the idea program was pushed so hard to get the two ideas per person per month or five ideas, that you ended up with a tip like put salt and pepper on the table in the cafeteria. The next one would be put a salt and pepper on every table in the cafeteria. We don't see that. We have a lot of great ideas. Our issue in large part is getting people to understand that it's okay to have a suggestion that's not implemented. It's okay to just comment on anything that you want just to move forward and to use it as a communication tool. I guess that's the part that I really can't emphasize enough, in other facilities I've been at, the suggestion system has failed because it was purely on how to make things improve. But I think if you use it as a communication tool, you're going to improve your overall process, not just your manufacturing process. In ours it is not at the two per person per month. I think if we counted those in team meetings and worked on that, we would be there but we haven't emphasized that, only because we get a huge number of very, very quality tips from our day-to-day system.

Suggested Reading List

Basadur, Min - *Simplex a Flight to Creativity* – Paperback Creative Education Foundation, 1995

Bodek, Norman – *Total Employee Involvement* – Handbook for Productivity Measurement and Improvement – (William F. Christopher and Carl G. Thor editors), Productivity Press – 1993, p 10-2.1

Covey, Stephen R. Covey – *The 7 Habits of Highly Effective People* – A Fireside Book, Simon & Schuster, 1989

De Bono, Edward - *Six Thinking Hats* - Little Brown & Co, 1999 paperback

De Bono, Edward - *Lateral Thinking: Creativity Step-By-Step* – HarperCollins, 1990

Deming, W. Edward - *Out of the Crisis* - MIT Press, 2000 paperback

Fisher, Kimbell - *Leading Self-Directed Work Teams: A Guide to Developing New Team Leadership Skills* - McGraw-Hill Professional Publishing, 1999

Fitz-Enz, Jac - *The 8 Practices of Exceptional Companies: How Great Organizations Make the Most of Their Human Assets* – AMACOM, 1997

Fitz-Enz, Jac - *The Roi of Human Capital: Measuring the Economic Value of Employee Performance* – AMACOM, 2000

Fitz-Enz, Jac and Jack J. Phillips - *A New Vision for Human Resources: Defining the Human Resources Function by Its Results* - Crisp Management Library, 1999

Fukuda, Ryuji – *Managerial Engineering: Techniques for Improving Quality and Productivity in the Workplace* – Productivity Press, 1983

Harrington H., James and Daryl Conner, Nicholas L. Horney - *Project Change Management : Applying Change Management to Improvement Projects* - McGraw-Hill Professional, 1999

Harrington H., James and Erik K. C. Esseling (Contributor), Harm Van Nimwegen - *Business Process Improvement Workbook : Documentation, Analysis, Design, and Management of Business Process Improvement* - McGraw-Hill Professional, 1997

Harrington H., James and Glen D. Hoffherr, Robert P. Reid - *The Creativity Toolkit: Provoking Creativity in Individuals and Organizations* – McGraw-Hill Professional,1998

Hall, Robert W. – *Attain Manufacturing Excellence* – McGraw-Hill Professional Publishing, 1988

Hutchins, Greg - *Iso 9000: A Comprehensive Guide to Registration, Audit Guidelines, and Successful Certification* - John Wiley & Sons, 1997

Hutchins, Greg - *Working It : The Rules Have Changed*: Y2K Edition - American Society for Quality, 1999

The Idea Generator – Quick and Easy Kaizen

Imai, Masaaki - *Kaizen: The Key to Japan's Competitive Success* – McGraw Hill, 1986

Jones, Morgan D. - *The Thinker's Toolkit : Fourteen Powerful Techniques for Problem Solving* - Times Books, 1998

Kaner, Sam and Lenny Lind, Catherine Toldi, Sarah Fisk, Duane Berger – *Facilitator's Guide to Participatory Decision-Making* - New Society Pub, 1996

Kelley, Tom with Jonathan Littman – *The Art of Innovation* – A Currency Book, published by Doubleday, 2001

King, Bob - *The Idea Edge: Transforming Creative Thought into Organizational Excellence* - Goal/Qpc, 1998

Laraia, Anthony C. and Patricia E. Moody, Robert W. Hall - *The Kaizen Blitz: Accelerating Breakthroughs in Productivity and Performance* – John Wiley & Sons, 1999

Liker, Jeffrey K., editor – *Becoming Lean* – Productivity Press, 1997

Maslow, Abraham, and Deborah C. Stephens, Gary Heil - *Maslow on Management* – John Wiley & Sons, 1998

McGregor, Douglas, and Warren G. Bennis – *Human Side of Enterprise: 25th Anniversary Printing – Japanese Manufacturing Techniques:* McGraw-Hill Higher Education, 1985

Moser-Wellman, Annette - *The Five Faces of Genius* – Viking Press 2001

Musashi, Miyamoto - *A Book of Five Rings* – (1584-1598) – The Classic Guide to Strategy – The Overlook Press, 1974

NKS/Factory Magazine - *Poka Yoke: Improving Product Quality by Preventing Defects* – Productivity Press,1988

Regan, Michael D. *The Kaizen Revolution* - Holden Press, 2000

Robinson, Alan G. and Sam Stern - *Corporate Creativity: How Innovation and Improvement Actually Happen* - Berrett-Koehler Pub, 1998

Schonberger, Richard J. – *Japanese Manufacturing Techniques: Nine Hidden Lessons in Simplicity* – Free Press, 1982

Schonberger, Richard J. – *World Class Manufacturing: The Next Decade* – Free Press, 1996

Schonberger, Richard J. – *The World Class Manufacturing: The Lessons of Simplicity Applied* – Free Press - 1986

Shingo, Shigeo - *A Revolution in Manufacturing: The SMED System* – Productivity Press, 1983

Shingo, Shigeo – *Zero Quality Control: Source Inspection and the Poka-yoke System* - Productivity Press, 1986

Sugiura, Tadashi and Yoshiaki Yamada – *The QC Storyline: A Guide to Solving Problems and Communicating the Results* – Asian Productivity Organization, 1995

The Idea Generator – Quick and Easy Kaizen

Suzaki, Kiyoshi - *The New Manufacturing Challenge: Techniques for Continuous Improvement* - Free Press, 1987

Tozawa, Bunji – *Kaizen Teian 1: Developing Systems for Continuous Improvement Through Employee Suggestions* – Productivity Press, 1992

Tozawa, Bunji – *Kaizen Teian 2: Developing Systems for Continuous Improvement Through Employee Suggestions* – Productivity Press, 1992

Tozawa, Bunji – T*he Idea Book: Improvement through TEI (Total Employee Involvement)* – Productivity Press, 1988

Tozawa, Bunji – *The Improvement Engine: Creativity & Innovation Through Employee Involvement* - Productivity Press – 1995

Tozawa, Bunji – *The Service Industry Idea Book: Employee Involvement in Retail and Office Improvement* – Productivity Press, 1990

Wellington, Patricia - *Kaizen Strategies for Customer Care: How to Create a Powerful Customer-Care Program—And Make It Work* –Financial Times Prentice Hall Publishing, 1996

Womack, James P. and Daniel T. Jones – *Lean Thinking, Banish Waste and Create Wealth in your Corporation* – Simon & Schuster, 1996

Bunji Tozawa – Biography

Education: Schooled in Kita, Kyushu, Japan. Graduate of Kagoshima University, Kagoshima, Japan, majored in Geology and Economics.

Professional Career: After college joined Kawasho Trading Company, a division of Kawasaki Steel. Twenty-five years later, in 1981, he joined The Japan HR Association as a writer. Today Mr. Tozawa is the CEO of The Japan HR Association, with offices in Tokyo and Osaka, Japan.

Instructor: Started to teach Kaizen in 1990 and has taught over 1000 seminars, now running approximately 120 three-hour seminars per year on Quick and Easy Kaizen throughout Southeast Asia. In Bangkok, Thailand, February 2001 he expected around 30 to 50 people for a seminar; 400 people arrived.

Publications:

Editor: Kaizen monthly magazine, Japan HR Association

Author of the following books:

PHP
Business Kaizen Techniques
Handbook of Kaizen OJT (On the Job Training)
Manual for Promoting Kaizen Activities

Sanno Daigaku Press
Through 5S with Kaizen

Simple Kaizen of Office Work
Marketing/Sales Kaizen

Asuka Press
Keys for Quick and Easy Kaizen of Work
Work Kaizen for Building a Strong Company

Kodansha Bunko
Kaizen in Cartoon Fashion

Kotsu-Shimbunsha
Successful Work Kaizen

Nikkankogyo-Shimbun
Defiant Work Kaizen
Kaizen Tale
Kaizen Q & A
Kaizen Promotion Starts with Examples and Ends with
Examples
Know-How of Quick & Easy Kaizen (3 Parts)
How to Make Kaizen (3 Parts)
Kaizen Teian (3 Parts)
Kaizen Reporting System
Kaizen Seminar Video Text

Gyosei
Work Kaizen Manual for Public Workers

Dojidaisha
Kaizen for Healthcare Workplace

Japan HR Association
Kaizen Teian Handbook

Service Kaizen Teian Handbook
Collection of Kaizen Examples

Consulting clients:
More than 230 companies including Shin-Etsu Chemical, Sony, Motorola, Sumitomo 3M, Matsushita Electric Industrial, Kyocera, Toyota, Roland, Chiba-Geigy, Yamaha Motor, Pioneer Electronic, Seiko Instruments, Epson

Norman Bodek - Biography

Education: University of Wisconsin, New York University (BA), and 42 additional credits at New York University Graduate School of Business, and New York University College of Education

Military service: Two years with the U. S. Army Audit Agency

Instructor: American Management Associations, Lecturer for Control Data Institute, President Regan's Productivity Conference – Washington, DC, PPORF Conference - Japan, Total Productive Maintenance Conference – Tokyo, Institute of Industrial Engineers, American Society for Quality, Productivity, Inc. Conferences and Seminars, Dresser Mfg., Union Carbide, AVCO Corporation, Larsen & Turbo, Productivity, Madras (Chenai), India, London - England, Jutland - Denmark

Recipient of The Shingo Prize[*] for Manufacturing Excellence run by Utah State University

Professional Career: Public Accountant, Vice President Data Utilities, New York City, President Key Universal Ltd. with offices in Greenwich, Connecticut and Grenada, West Indies

1979-1999 Started Productivity Inc. & Productivity Press:

---

[*]For information on the prize: 65 http://www.shingoprize.org/shingo/index.html

Newsletters: PRODUCTIVITY, Total Employee Involvement (TEI), The Service Insider, Quick Change Over (QCO), and Total Productive Maintenance (TPM)

Study missions to Japan, led around 35 missions visiting 250 manufacturing plants

Conferences: Over 100 conferences on productivity and quality improvement including Productivity The American Way, Best of America, Quality, Quality Service, TPM, TEI

Seminars: Hundreds of seminars on TPM, TQM, TEI, QCO, Visual Management, 5S, JIT and others.

In plant training events: Five Days and One Night (now called Kaizen Blitz), Maintenance Miracle, and benchmark plant visits and seminars with American Manufacturing companies.

Published: Dr. Shigeo Shingo's - Toyota Production System, SMED, Poka-Yoke, Non-Stock Production, etc., Taiichi Ohno - Toyota Production System (JIT), Henry Ford – Today and Tomorrow, A New American TQM, Yoji Akao – Quality Function Deployment (QFD) and Hoshin Kanri, Dr. Ryuji Fukuda – Managerial Engineering, CEDAC and Building Organizational Fitness, Shigeichi Moriguchi – Software Excellence, Shigeru Mizuno - Management for Quality Improvement (The 7 New QC Tools), Seiichi Nakajima – Total Productivity Maintenance (TPM), Michel Greif – The Visual Factory, Ken'ichi Sekine – One Piece Flow, Shigehiro Nakamura – The New Standardization, and many other books on world class manufacturing and total quality management.

1990 - Industry Week called him "Mr. Productivity"

1999 - Started Perfect Customer Service with a monthly newsletter, consulting, and workshops on Quick and Easy Kaizen and Improving Customer Service

The Idea Generator – Quick and Easy Kaizen

Writings: Numerous editorials and articles on productivity, quality and customer service.

Exhibits

The Idea Generator – Quick and Easy Kaizen

Illustration List

The Idea Generator – Quick and Easy Kaizen

INDEX